Assessing the
International Forest Regime

IUCN - The World Conservation Union

Founded in 1948, The World Conservation Union brings together States, government agencies and a diverse range of non-governmental organizations in a unique world partnership: over 930 members in all, spread across some 138 countries.

As a Union, IUCN seeks to influence, encourage and assist societies throughout the world to conserve the integrity and diversity of nature and to ensure that any use of natural resources is equitable and ecologically sustainable. A central secretariat coordinates the IUCN Programme and serves the Union membership, representing their views on the world stage and providing them with the strategies, services, scientific knowledge and technical support they need to achieve their goals. Through its six Commissions, IUCN draws together over 6,000 expert volunteers in project teams and action groups, focusing in particular on species and biodiversity conservation and the management of habitats and natural resources. The Union has helped many countries to prepare National Conservation Strategies, and demonstrates the application of its knowledge through the field projects it supervises. Operations are increasingly decentralized and are carried forward by an expanding network of regional and country offices, located principally in developing countries.

The World Conservation Union builds on the strengths of its members, networks and partners to enhance their capacity and to support global alliances to safeguard natural resources at local, regional and global levels.

Assessing the
International Forest Regime

Edited by

Richard G. Tarasofsky

IUCN Environmental Policy and Law Paper No. 37

IUCN - The World Conservation Union
1999

The designation of geographical entities in this book, and the presentation of the material, do not imply the expression of any opinion whatsoever on the part of IUCN concerning the legal status of any country, territory, or area, or of its authorities, or concerning the delimitation of its frontiers or boundaries.

The views expressed in this publication do not necessarily reflect those of IUCN or its members.

Published by:	IUCN, Gland, Switzerland and Cambridge, UK in collaboration with IUCN Environmental Law Centre, Bonn, Germany.

Citation:	Richard G. Tarasofsky (1999). *Assessing the International Forest Regime*. IUCN, Gland, Switzerland, Cambridge, UK and Bonn, Germany. xii + 156 pp.
ISBN:	2-8317-0472-3
Cover design by:	IUCN Environmental Law Centre
Cover photograph:	Mixed forest in autumn colours, Pechoro Ilych Nature Reserve, Russia: Per Angelstau
Layout by:	Barbara Weiner, Desktop Publications Co-ordinator
Printed by:	Daemisch Mohr, Siegburg, Germany
Available from:	IUCN Publications Services Unit 219c Huntingdon Road, Cambridge CB3 0DL, United Kingdom Tel: +44 1223 277894, Fax: +44 1223 277175 E-mail: info@books.iucn.org www: http://www.iucn.org A catalogue of IUCN publications is also available

IUCN wishes to acknowledge the financial support for this project provided by the John D. and Catherina T. MacArthur Foundation.

Table of Contents

The Conservation and Sustainable Use of Forest Biological Diversity: the Role of the Convention on Biological Diversity
Ruth Khalastchi and Ruth Mackenzie

Global Forest Policy and Selected International Instruments: a Preliminary Review
David R. Downes

Global Cooperation on Forests through International Institutions
Richard G. Tarasofsky and David R. Downes

Regional Legal Arrangements for Forests: the Case of Central America
Grethel Aguilar and Marco González

Foreword

Assessing the International Forest Regime is the second IUCN publication to deal with the international law on forests. In 1995, *The International Forest Regime – Legal and Policy Issues*, also by Richard G. Tarasofsky, was published by IUCN and WWF. In the Foreword to that publication, Don Gilmour and I wrote:

> The decision to establish the Intergovernmental Panel on Forests (IPF) comes at a time when the political environment seems ready to consider future directions in global forest policy. At no time in the past several years has the prospect of making significant progress seemed so bright. The IPF – dealing with an issue long plagued by political divisions, especially between developed and developing countries – represents an opportunity to develop a real global consensus.

With hindsight, those words seem overly optimistic. Although the IPF was successful in resolving some issues, many of the fundamental divisions linger on. In particular, the thorny debate over a possible convention on forests has proven very difficult to resolve.

Shortly after this book is printed, an intersessional process will begin to support Category III of the work programme of the Intergovernmental Forum on Forests (i.e. international arrangements and mechanisms to promote the management, conservation and sustainable development of all types of forests). I will be a little more circumspect in this Foreword as to the outcome of this process. While a process which examines these issues in a comprehensive and open-ended fashion can be useful, it is too soon to say whether the methodology adopted will yield the desired outcome.

But it is clear that some decision about a new legal instrument needs to be taken. One of the clear findings of this book is that the persistence of the current divide is very counterproductive to the development of existing instruments. Yet the issue is complex and decision-makers face a serious dilemma. The current situation is not sufficient, and yet going ahead with a new instrument brings with it several risks.

From the outset, IUCN, which is neutral on the issue of a new convention, has been concerned about the high level of rhetoric surrounding this debate. Our approach since the commencement of the IFF has been to inject a technical perspective into the deliberations. Regardless of whatever decision about a new instrument is ultimately taken, more synergies at all levels need to be developed between relevant legal instruments and international institutions. This need is already very present; a new instrument will naturally make this even more so. I hope this book will provide a useful basis on which to evaluate the need for a new instrument and to help build these badly-needed synergies.

Françoise Burhenne-Guilmin
Head, IUCN Environmental Law Centre
Bonn, Germany

Acknowledgements

I am grateful for the contributions of all the authors, each of whom worked much longer and harder than originally anticipated. I am also grateful to Bill Jackson, Simon Rietbergen, Carole St. Laurent, Andrea Finger, Christian Mersmann and Andrew Deutz for their insightful comments on earlier drafts. Thanks to all those who participated in IUCN's open forum held at IFF-2 in Geneva in August 1998, for their constructive critique of the authors' first drafts. Thanks also go to the various people involved in the international forest policy process who provided me with useful information and other encouragement. Bill Mankin and colleagues at IUCN-US were very helpful in helping to attract funding for this project. At the ELC, the preparation of this book benefited from the guidance of Françoise Burhenne-Guilmin and the assistance of Ann DeVoy. Barbara Weiner maintained her good humour while doing the typesetting under hectic circumstances. Finally, the financial support for this project from the John D. and Catherine T. MacArthur Foundation is gratefully acknowledged.

Richard G. Tarasofsky
Berlin, Germany
22 January 1999

List of Contributors

Grethel Aguilar (Costa Rica) is a lawyer and a private consultant, as well as the Vice Chair for Mesoamerica of the IUCN Commission on Environmental Law.

David R. Downes (USA) is a Senior Attorney with the Centre for International Environmental Law in Washington, D.C.

Marco Gonzáles (Nicaragua) is a lawyer and Director of the Environmental Law Programme of the Central American Commission on Environment and Development.

Ruth Khalastchi (United Kingdom) is a Staff Lawyer at the Foundation for International Environmental Law and Development (FIELD), Managing Editor of the Review of European Community and International Environmental Law (RECIEL) and Visiting Lecturer in Law at the School of Oriental and African Studies (SOAS), University of London.

Ruth Mackenzie (United Kingdom) is Programme Director of the Biodiversity and Marine Resources Programme at FIELD and Lecturer in Law at SOAS, University of London.

Dr. Astrid Skala-Kuhmann (Germany) is a lawyer who works as an independent consultant for the Government of Germany and GTZ on international legal issues relating to forests.

Richard G. Tarasofsky (Canada) is a Senior Associate of the IUCN Environmental Law Centre and of Ecologic - Centre for International and European Environmental Policy. He was the manager of this project.

Assessing the International Forest Regime: Gaps, Overlaps, Uncertainties and Opportunities

By Richard G. Tarasofsky

I.   Introduction

This book provides an assessment of the international forest regime,[1] in response to calls from many quarters, including the UN Intergovernmental Forum on Forests (IFF) and the World Commission on Forests and Sustainable Development, as well as from several non-governmental organizations (NGOs). Such an analysis is necessary for its own sake, to determine the effectiveness of the present regime, but also to assess the need for any new legal instruments.

The focus of the book is mainly on action taken by countries at the global level, in the framework of legally binding instruments and institutions.[2] It builds on previous analyses of the international forest regime by looking beyond the legal mandates so to begin exploring the actual performance of the components against their mandates. This examination is done from several perspectives. With the Intergovernmental Panel on Forests (IPF) Proposals for Action as the point of departure, the effectiveness and impact of individual legal instruments and global institutions are analysed, as is the potential for synergy between them. In addition, a regional case study is presented.

The remainder of this chapter will begin by outlining the main options and dilemmas facing those examining the possible reform of the existing regime. It will then review the main findings of the other chapters in this volume, before proceeding to make findings and observations that relate to the current intergovernmental process.

II.   Options and Dilemmas

It is beyond dispute that current international forest regime, as a whole, is not having the effect it should. It is not creating the conditions for national, sub-national and private actors to ensure the conservation, sustainable management and sustainable development of all types of forests. It does not sufficiently provide for the means for achieving this objective, for example:

- clear rules and measurable standards;
- appropriate financing and positive incentives;
- technology transfer;
- consensus on a bottom-up and holistic approach;
- coordination between institutions and policies at all levels;
- a permanent forum for dialogue and equitable resolution of conflicts.

Does this mean that the only solution is a new global convention on forests? It is argued in some quarters that the fragmentation of the international forest regime is such that a new convention on forests is the best means to establish coherence. However, this matter is rather complex.

IUCN – The World Conservation Union is neither for nor against the *per se* establishment of a new convention. Rather its primary concern is the conservation of the integrity and diversity of nature and the use of natural resources in a manner that is equitable and ecologically sustainable, and therefore is in favour of an international forest regime which most effectively supports this end,

---

[1]   Regime in this context means the totality of norms, rules, standards and procedures, as expressed in international instruments and other acts.

[2]   Regional initiatives, such as those that are developing criteria and indicators for sustainable forest management, are not covered here, although they impact on the development of the global regime.

whatever the form. That said, IUCN cannot be oblivious to the risks of undertaking negotiations on a new legal instrument at this time:

- The complex negotiations will be lengthy, and consume significant financial and technical resources from all countries – thereby possibly slowing much needed action on the ground. Even if a new instrument is adopted, it may not enter into force quickly, while effective implementation will take even longer.

- The divisions within the international community may lead to a weak set of norms reflecting the lowest common denominator. This risk is particularly significant given the current lack of substantive global consensus on key issues.

- A new instrument may undermine the efforts being taken under the myriad of other instruments and institutions that deal with forest issues.

It is not as if these risks cannot be overcome – they can. But their significance suggests that there is an onus on those advocating a new convention to demonstrate that such an exercise will indeed be worthwhile.

Indeed, a more constructive approach is for matters of substance to be the point of departure. Once effective solutions to forest-related problems are identified, it is then possible to consider vehicles for delivering these solutions: e.g. legal instruments and international institutions. Given that we are not beginning from a legal or institutional void – far from it – a key criterion for selecting among the various options is the extent to which they support a synergistic relationship with what already exists. A second, perhaps even more significant, criterion is how conducive the options are to effective implementation on the ground, given the reality that political will to make actual change tends to be less than it ought to be. As the World Commission on Forests and Sustainable Development puts it:

> ... there is a crisis of credibility given the myriad [of] international legal agreements that await serious implementation, which could bring significant dividends to forests, and given that the global compact based on one earth, one world, a common future envisaged in the Earth Summit, is far from being a political reality.[3]

Although one may intuitively concur with the World Commission's opinion, the international forest regime is complex, where both successes and failures regarding implementation have taken place. An objective analysis of which aspects of precisely which treaties and programmes are having an impact, and why or why not, would be very useful indeed. Indeed, it is hoped that this book will provide a basis for this next necessary phase of analysis.

Finally, it must be emphasised that even perfect international legal instruments and institutions will not be sufficient in themselves to bring about the necessary change. These entities are inherently flawed by the fact that they tend not to involve all the major stakeholders in a meaningful way. By focusing mainly on the governmental level, especially for the formulation of their mandates, but also for their implementation, the traditional international legal system is not conducive for creating the effective public-private partnerships that are essential for dealing with current forest problems. Indeed, it is sobering to consider that despite the lack of progress at the international policy level, some elements of the private sector have proceeded to break new ground by giving effect to norms which are still "emerging" at the governmental level.

---

[3] World Commission on Forests and Sustainable Development, Our Forests ... Our Future, Summary of Draft Report Prepared for the IFF, 24 August – 4 September 1998, at p. 23.

III. Reviewing the Current International Forest Regime

The following draws on and builds upon some key points made by the contributors to this book. A more exhaustive treatment of each of these issues, and others, is to be found in the individual chapters.

1. Moving Forward from the IPF Proposals for Action

Astrid Skala-Kuhmann's chapter on "Implementation of the IPF Proposals for Action in Light of Relevant International Legally-Binding Instruments", builds on recent discussions within the IFF, including the Six-Country Initiative on Putting the IPF Proposals into Action. It is a first step towards examining how synergies in implementation can be built between the IPF Proposals and international treaties that impact on forests.

Prima facie, the IPF Proposals for Action can, in principle, provide helpful guidance in the implementation of relevant treaties, since these treaties tend to contain general obligations of result rather than detailed instructions on how these results are to be achieved. However desirable this potential for synergy might appear to be, in reality there are at least three key obstacles to achieving it. The first is that the IPF Proposals themselves are not always explicit as to how they relate to existing instruments. Secondly, many of the IPF Proposals are neither specific enough nor reflect a true international consensus so as to be easily implementable. Third, several treaties are currently at early stages of implementation and key points of controversy in the IPF are also reflected in these instruments.

There is, however, enough of a basis to begin building synergies. As such, *Dr. Skala-Kuhmann* makes a number of recommendations aimed at national and international levels. Because many of actions required for achieving the necessary synergies are country-specific, national forest programmes (NFPs), or their equivalent should be the organising framework for implementation of the IPF Proposals and relevant treaty obligations. This will entail, as first step, coordinating NFPs with the treaty requirements to prepare national biodiversity and desertification strategies, as well as national strategies to deal with climate change. Meanwhile, at the international level, governing bodies of relevant treaties and institutions should focus more clearly on how they should relate to each other, and should provide increased guidance and support for synergistic implementation. Other key actions to be done at the national level include coordinating information and reporting systems, so as to support a more coordinated approach at the international level.

2. Existing Instruments and Institutions

The approach taken in this book is to examine all relevant global instruments and institutions so as to identify, where possible, the following:

- The mandate of each institution and its relationship to the conservation and sustainable management of forests;

- The forest and forestry-related programmes and the human and financial resources for these programmes;

- The strength and weakness of each institution with respect to matters such as the technical expertise of staff, financial resources, and political support for its mandate;

- The potential for future success and the identification of obstacles that might block progress on implementation of forest-related programs or obligations.

2.1 International Legal Instruments

The *Convention on Biological Diversity* (CBD) is the subject of an entire chapter of the book. This is because, as the authors, *Ruth Khalastchi and Ruth Mackenzie*, themselves affirm, the scope of the CBD is such that it.could encompass most, if not all, issues relating to the conservation and sustainable use of forests. However, the nature of the CBD – i.e. not being self-executing – and the design of its mechanisms mean that sufficient political will and commitment at both national and international levels is necessary give effect to its full legal promise. The history of the debate on forests within the CBD reveals that obstacles at various stages have prevented the harnessing of this will.

Some of these obstacles have to do with differing visions among Parties about the convention itself, while others have to do with the fact that the relationship between the CBD and the IPF/IFF has not been fully defined. This latter ambiguity has, to some extent, led to a kind of perverse "competition" between the two, where progress in one is prevented by the existence of the other. It is also the case that the fundamental disagreement about the desirability of a new convention on forests has had the unfortunate result of some countries preventing the CBD from developing to its full potential, for fear that this might undermine their case.

The main output in relation to forests of the CBD process so far is the work programme on forest biodiversity. But the content of this programme – in that it concentrates mainly on information gathering, research and coordination, rather than substantive measures – is not action-oriented (at least in its first phase), again reflecting the fundamental ambiguities surrounding the role of the CBD. It remains to be seen how effective this work programme will be, given that there is no explicit role laid out for the secretariat and given that the Conference of the Parties (COP) has declined so far to establish a technical panel on forest issues. Although the CBD COP will review progress made on its various thematic work programmes at its next meeting in 2000, the COP will only pay particular focus to forest biodiversity at its 6th meeting, which will take place only in 2001 or 2002, i.e. after the UN Commission on Sustainable Development (CSD) will decide, in 2000, how to follow up on the IFF. This may mean that the CBD will be restricted to a reactive role to whatever is decided by the IFF or the CSD.

David R. Downes examines the remaining global treaties that impact on forests. He begins by considering the *Ramsar Convention* and the *World Heritage Convention*, which impact on the conservation of forests. Both these are shown to be useful, and indeed could be made even more so, but it must be emphasised that even in the best case scenario they will only apply to a relatively small class of forests – mangroves in the former case and forests of outstanding natural or cultural value in the latter. *UNESCO's Biosphere Reserves*, also examined here, are similarly useful instruments, but again limited in scope.

A strong basis for defining equitable rights for indigenous peoples who are forest dwellers or otherwise connected to forests is to be found in *International Labour Organization (ILO) Convention 169*. So far, however, that instrument has not attracted universal support – in fact only a handful of countries are party to it. Another weakness is that it sits uneasily in the framework of the ILO, whose main programme is substantively different. The *Draft UN Declaration on the Rights of Indigenous Peoples* may help to build support for certain key norms, but it is not at all obvious at this stage that the final version of the Declaration will contain sufficiently powerful provisions. The CBD may ultimately prove to be the most effective venue for defining the rights of indigenous forest dwellers, .e.g. through its recently created open-ended working group, although it is still too soon to tell. It must be recalled, however, that the wording of Article 8(j), which addresses indigenous matters, heavily qualifies these rights by making them subject to national legislation.

The examination of the international trading regime suggests some mixed results for forests. On the one hand, some positive synergies may exist between trade liberalisation and the conservation, sustainable management and sustainable development of forests. On the other hand, it is evident that trade liberalisation can exacerbate the effects of unsustainable management practices in a variety of ways. The legal instruments and institutions only provide a partial answer. Indeed, the debate within the **World Trade Organization** (WTO) on its relationship to the environment, which is far from over, reveals considerable differences between members. Where the WTO has taken clear decisions regarding the environment, primarily in its dispute settlement body, the results have not been favourable to environmental conservation. Furthermore, concerns persist that voluntary incentives for sustainable forest management, such as certification and labelling under the Forest Stewardship Council, may be ruled inconsistent with the WTO. It must be stressed that at present the WTO itself has no specialisation in forest issues and neither do the member representatives tend to have any capacity in this regard, and therefore does not have the capacity to deal with these issues on its own. Nonetheless, by virtue of its active dispute settlement system, the WTO may soon be faced with these issues, i.e. before a normative basis for resolving these conflicts has been fully developed. A more appropriate solution would be to craft a constructive relationship between the WTO and other international environmental instruments and institutions, including those which belong to the international forest regime.

Uncertainty about consistency with the WTO rules also exists in relation to trade measures taken under multilateral environmental agreements. One such agreement, the **Convention on International Trade in Endangered Species of Wild Fauna and Flora** (CITES), is considered an effective tool at controlling trade in endangered species threatened by trade, as well as providing a useful framework for managed trade in species which risk becoming threatened by trade. Although CITES has been applied to tree and woody species, this has not happened consistently or to the Convention's full potential. Nonetheless, the positive experience with the Convention's Timber Working Group suggests that CITES may become more significant for forests in the future, once its full potential to contribute to both conservation and sustainable trade are more widely appreciated.

The **Kyoto Protocol to the Climate Change Convention**, once in force, ought to lead to more forests being conserved and sustainably used. However, this promise must be put into perspective. Firstly, the approach to forests will be based primarily on only one of many values: i.e. how well they store carbon. Secondly, instruments like the Clean Development Mechanism and "joint implementation" will not operate in all countries with forest cover. Secondly, there are still several fundamental controversies to work out before these instruments become operational. These include the definition of terms like "reforestation", the measurement of baselines, and unexpected "leakage" from projects. It is also not at all clear what the impact on forests of tradable emissions rights will be. Similarly, overall potential of the Kyoto Protocol diminishing the adverse impact of climate change on forests is also clouded by several uncertainties.

By contrast, the challenges faced by the **Desertification Convention** do not tend to include definitional issues, but rather very practical ones. This Convention has considerable potential to assist countries affected by desertification and drought to develop a sustainable ecosystem approach to managing their forests, and other natural resources. Its holistic and grassroots-oriented approach is ambitious and will require a significant financial investment in order to be effective.

2.2 International Institutions

Richard Tarasofsky and David Downes examine several international institutions relating to forests. Some of these institutions are members of the **Interagency Task Force on Forests** (ITFF), which was created to support the work of the IPF. Although the ITFF has been a forum for international organisations to meet, and even build partnerships around the IPF Programme Elements, it cannot yet be asserted that it is a comprehensive coordinating mechanism.

Several institutions appear to have recently been, or currently are, at critical turning points. The *UN Food and Agriculture Organization* (FAO) is one such example. Prior to the UN Conference on Environment and Development (UNCED) it held an uncontested leadership role in international policy development, however, several controversies undermined its credibility in the early 1990s. Nonetheless, the FAO remains a critical actor, not least because it is the task manager in the UN System for Chapter 11 of Agenda 21, but also because it has reformed significantly over the past few years. In particular, the FAO's reorientation in support of National Forest Programmes is significant, given the central role advocated for such programmes by the IPF. The FAO also has considerable technical resources to provide legal assistance, information dissemination, and analysis, although these resources pale in comparison with other FAO programmes. The FAO Committee on Forestry (COFO) may no longer be the central intergovernmental arena for global policy discussions on forests, but as the multilateral forum underpinning the FAO work on forests, it has the potential to send out wider policy signals. In addition, with the FAO's regional forestry commissions and its field-level work, the depth of the FAO's reach surpasses other institutions. A key challenge facing the FAO, and indeed the larger international community, is in how best to define its niche and role in relation to other international instruments and institutions relating to forests. This challenge may become more acute once the IFF ends.

The *International Tropical Timber Organization* (ITTO) has also reoriented itself following the entry into force in 1997 of the 1994 International Tropical Timber Agreement (ITTA). While some of the ITTO's early work was pioneering from the conceptual standpoint, its potential contribution to sustainable forest management suffers from at least two factors. The first is that it is primarily a commodity trade organisation limited to only a portion of global trade and, secondly, the ITTA 1994 was the subject of particularly acrimonious negotiations. The ITTO has recently produced some useful policy guidelines and has adopted its Objective 2000 – "enhancing the capacity of members to implement a strategy for achieving exports of tropical timber and timber products from sustainably managed sources by the year 2000". But the Organization has been previously criticised for not being able to ensure implementation of these policy developments on the ground. Nonetheless, the creation of the Bali Partnership fund to support the Objective 2000 is a positive step, and so too are some aspects of the recently adopted Libreville Action Plan. Again, though, it remains to be seen how these will be translated into practice. The ITTO has an important technical role to play, which if properly harnessed, can help steer the tropical timber trade in a more sustainable direction. At the same time, though, for the reasons mentioned above, it cannot be expected that the ITTO will be the venue where global trade and environment issues relating to forests will be decided, even though the ITTO is the lead agency for this topic in the IFF.

The *UN Development Programme's* (UNDP) work on forests is largely technical in nature. However, its recently established Programme on Forests can be expected to contribute to the better understanding of public-private partnerships for sustainable forest management, strategies, NFPs, and innovative financial mechanisms. This latter topic will usefully contribute to UNDP's work at the IFF on financing issues, for which it is the lead agency. A key strength of UNDP's approach is that it conducts activities at both the field and international levels – with the appropriate feedback loops in place, this can be a powerful combination. UNDP also is strong in providing capacity-building, through its Forest Capacity Programme. Perhaps a key challenge for UNDP, in addition to attracting sufficient financial, as well as political, support for its Programme on Forests, is to effectively reconcile its development-centred approach with the ecological values of forests not associated with direct human use and consumption.

The *UN Environment Programme* (UNEP) has a relatively modest programme on forests, and given its "catalytic role", it mostly undertakes activities in partnership with other organisations and initiatives. Although much of the work is technical, e.g. participating in the development of regional criteria and indicators, UNEP also has an important conceptual role to play. Strengthened by the fact that UNEP usefully integrates its forest-related work into its broader biodiversity programme, which may allow it to create some interesting policy linkages, it is also the lead organisation in ITFF for examining the underlying causes of deforestation. However, this topic is enormous, and whether UNEP's actual impact will be significant may largely depend upon the financial and technical resources available to it. It also remains to be seen whether UNEP's recent restructuring activities will help raise its effectiveness in relation to forests.

The **World Bank's** role in assisting developing countries in relation to conservation and management of forests is certainly significant if only by virtue of its massive spending power, although it must be noted that the allocation for forest-related work is relatively small. However, the Bank's record has been criticised from several perspectives. Firstly, there are concerns that notwithstanding its 1991 Forest Policy, it has not taken a sufficiently cross-sectoral approach to lessening the pressures on forests (including from sectors where it also provides significant funding). A second concern is the breadth and depth of the consultation procedures with interested and affected parties. Thirdly, it has failed to mainstream global environmental values, such as biodiversity, into it work. However, the Bank has recently undertaken some interesting initiatives, such as its alliance with WWF on protected areas and certification that may prove fruitful. Finally, the Bank is currently reviewing its 1991 Forest Policy, which may lead to a more effective deployment of its human, technical and financial resources.

The **Global Environment Facility** (GEF), as the financial mechanism of the CBD and FCCC, is of critical importance not only in relation to the goals of those treaties, but also because it has an operational programme concerning forests. Although the amount of funding available under the GEF was considered by the recent independent evaluation to be small in relation to needs, the GEF has been successful in leveraging significant amounts of cofinancing.

The potential for the **International Monetary Fund's** structural adjustment programs to adversely affect forests is briefly noted. Although general points are made about some potentially negative impacts of such programs on forests, this was an area where further research is necessary.

3. Focusing on the regional perspective

The final chapter of the book reviews the one region in the world that has a legally binding instrument on forests which is in operation, namely, Central America. While the authors of this chapter, *Grethel Aguilar and Marco Gonzáles*, identify some successes which the **Central America Forest Convention** can be credited with, it is clear that there are some unique factors in that region that help make this so. One is the overall drive and commitment to regional integration on a host of environment and development issues, which has enjoyed a high political profile. Indeed, the Central American Forest Convention is to be understood as part of a wider web of legal instruments and institutions – and indeed it itself was only developed after a solid legal and institutional foundation had been laid. Secondly, the countries of the region are sufficiently like-minded in their evolving approach to the management of forests, which involves using incentive measures, rather than simply command-and-control.

Thirdly, a defining feature of the Central American process has been the heavy involvement of civil society in the decision-making. The institutions created by the Central American Forest Convention, and the other regional environmental treaties, have made meaningful engagement with relevant stakeholders a priority, with the result that working partnerships have been cultivated. In some cases, these institutions have even facilitated the creation of civil-society groups with whom it can have dialogue. Given that Central America has used regional treaties to implement global norms in a regionally-specific manner, it stands out as a useful model for building synergies between these norms in a constructively participatory manner. This has proven particularly important in the case of forests, which ultimately requires the buy-in of non-State actors if viable solutions are to be found. This is certainly so in Central America, but also elsewhere.

IV. Findings

Given the lack of certainty about the true impact of the current regime, and that it is fluid and continuously evolving, it is difficult to precisely identify gaps, overlaps and opportunities. Nonetheless, some findings are possible.

1. Gaps

If one considers gaps as lacunae in the law or in the spectrum of institutional mandates as regards their coverage of important forest issues or problems, then several exist in the current international forest regime, although they are of different orders of scale. Of particular importance is that several key underlying causes of deforestation are not covered: e.g. agrarian land reform in relation to landless peasants, environmental aspects of mining, and activities of transnational corporations. Another, perhaps more manageable, gap is the lack of an international mechanism to control illegal trade in forest products. This would be a fairly straightforward matter to address through international law – e.g. through universal agreement on permitting and control schemes. However, this has so far not been attempted.

2. Overlaps

This book points out some areas where overlaps between the mandates of more than one instrument or institution exist. However, one should not overemphasise the dangers of overlaps, since they, like their mandates, tend to be at the general level. For example, the World Heritage, Ramsar and CBD all cover forest conservation, but each instrument and institution has its own specialised perspective, which can be valuable. The real challenge is to find synergy on the ground in a manner that brings out the strength of each instrument or programme. But this is a challenge that can be overcome, as suggested in the following chapter in this book. Thus, the various requirements to develop national strategies, plans and programmes should be linked where appropriate, the onus being on countries themselves to determine how best these should implemented in their particular contexts. At the international level, it should also be possible to coordinate obligations relating to technology transfer, information exchange and research.

3. Uncertainties

This book reveals that there are certain important aspects of the international forest regime that are uncertain. At the conceptual level, a key one is international trade, where there currently appears to be significant potential for clashes between rules and principles for trade and those for sustainable development. A second type of uncertainty arises from differences of opinion about the actual meaning of norms or how they should be implemented. One example is the amount of financing that should be provided by the North to the South. Another relates to the entitlements of indigenous peoples dependent on forests. These are fundamental matters; uncertainty about them diminishes the political credibility of the overall regime, and impacts on the ability of national forest authorities to raise the position of forests on the national agenda. However, not all uncertainties are equally problematic. For example, the uncertainty created by the lack of definitions of key concepts, such as "conservation", "sustainable management" and "sustainable development", may not be such a large problem in practice, as discussed below.

4. Opportunities

The current international forest regime offers considerable opportunity for enhancement in terms of substance, effectiveness of delivery, and synergy among the various instruments and institutions. All the instruments and institutions surveyed here tend to be living entities that have the capacity to evolve in these directions. Indeed, virtually all of the gaps and uncertainties identified in this book *can*, from the legal point of view, be resolved within the existing framework. The key is marshalling sufficient political will to make this happen. As suggested below, harnessing this political will requires more than simply engaging government officials who deal with forest issues, but a more cross-sectoral input with heavy buy-in from civil society.

V. Final Observations

This book helps demonstrate that there is still much the existing regime can offer, if it was effectively implemented. This requires more political will than that which exists to date. Indeed those advocating a new convention must recognise that while a legal instrument helps leverage some political will to implement it, the amount is rarely sufficient on its own. The experience with the Central American Convention is cautionary – while it is considered to be a qualified success, it has not halted deforestation in that region.

The lack of effective implementation may also reveal the limits of government action. Although governments play a critical role in defining and enforcing rules and standards, they alone cannot achieve conservation, sustainable management and sustainable development of all forests. As globalization has gathered pace in this last decade, industry, communities, NGOs, and individuals have increased in importance relative to the public sector. This is not to say that the empowerment of non-State actors has been uniform or equitable – far from it. But what is now clear is that public/private partnerships are needed, as are incentives and clear "rules of the game" for members of civil society to take positive action in relation to forests. The role of law is to create the framework conditions for this to happen, which includes, in part, regulating these new power relations. The failure to attract sufficient political will is a failure to involve all relevant sectors of society in setting a common vision for forests – in part this is to be understood as a failure in the national and international legal systems in setting the stage for this to happen.

The existing regime is rich, but fragmented. Key gaps and uncertainties remain. A stronger and more cohesive regime is necessary, especially one which focuses and supports implementation. It is tempting to think that the only solution is a holistic convention on forests. While in ideal circumstances a convention can help achieve the objective of the international forest regime, in reality the risks, as outlined above, are significant.

At the same time, the prospect of the international forest policy process being endlessly paralysed over the "convention" debate, will mean that "business as usual" (i.e. continuing deforestation) will continue to operate in the vacuum. There can be little doubt that this will mean the continued devastating rate of deforestation, and therefore a tremendous failure of the international forest regime. Thus, the IFF must not be distracted by this debate, but should, as a first and urgent priority, forge substantive consensus on the actions necessary to achieve the conservation, sustainable management and sustainable development of all forests. This involves, at the very least, elaborating concepts that will bridge the gaps identified here and resolve the persisting uncertainties. It cannot be expected that the IFF alone can operationalise these concepts, but a strong and clear message from the IFF will be influential.

To succeed in facilitating this consensus-building process the IFF will have to set priorities, so that it can focus on matters that are truly pressing. In so doing, it is not advisable for it to deal with issues that are still largely abstract. For example, while the lack of definitions of key terms create uncertainties and possibly contribute to the fragmented nature of the international forest regime, the time may not yet be ripe to undertake definitional exercises. These are concepts that need to be informed by actual experience over time, including with the application of criteria and indicators.

Finally, in dealing with Category III of its work programme (i.e. international arrangements and mechanisms to promote the management, conservation and sustainable development of all types of forests), the members of the IFF must come to closure on the debate about new legal instruments. However, this discussion should not continue to take place at the current level of abstraction and theory. Therefore, it is recommended that the IFF should:

- accelerate the systematic examination of the effectiveness of the international forest regime, focusing particularly on impacts on the ground;

- examine the feasibility of existing international instruments and institutions to address the gaps and uncertainties in the current regime; and

- examine the feasibility of mechanisms, in addition to a new convention, to achieve the necessary coordination at the international level.

Implementation of the IPF Proposals for Action in Light of Relevant International Legally-Binding Instruments

By Astrid Skala-Kuhmann

I. Introduction

1. Objective and Background

The purpose of the paper is to examine the linkages and synergies between the implementation of the Intergovernmental Panel on Forests (IPF) Proposals for Action (hereinafter "IPF Proposals") and existing forest-related international legal instruments. In particular, the paper will identify these linkages and synergies and recommend ways to implement them in a mutually supportive manner.

The IPF noted the importance of finding linkages between the Panel's work and existing international legal instruments relevant to forests, and which was seen as helping to develop a coherent and consistent, holistic and balanced approach to the management and conservation of all types of forests. This was based on the mandate of the IPF, which recognized the need to

> ... develop a clearer view of the work being carried out ... under existing instruments as appropriate, including the Convention on Biological Diversity et al., in order to identify any gaps, areas requiring enhancement, as well as any areas of duplication.[1]

During the IPF discussions, the need to analyse existing international instruments to determine the gaps, overlaps, duplication and inter-linkages in the present international forest regime was emphasized. This was seen as particularly important given the mandate to explore the necessity of a legally binding instrument covering all types of forests.[2] Although the IPF in its Final Report[3] elaborated several conclusions and adopted six Proposals for Action concerning Programme Element V on "International organizations and multilateral institutions and instruments, including appropriate legal mechanisms", the need to examine existing instruments was left pending. It was thus incorporated into the Programme of Work of the Intergovernmental Forum on Forests (IFF) Programme Element II.e, on "Forest-related work of international and regional organizations, and under existing instruments", and Category III, on "International arrangements and mechanisms to promote the management, conservation and sustainable development of all types of forests."

The analysis of existing instruments is surely necessary in order engage in exploring further improvement of the international forest regime, and even more so to set the framework for a substantive discussion on a legally-binding instrument covering all types of forests. But at the same time, there seems an increasing need to explore the existing forest-related instruments from a different angle: the effectiveness of their implementation concerning forest-related objectives. Indeed, the importance of focusing on actual implementation was acknowledged by the IFF during its Second Session, whose Report urges an in-depth analysis of the experiences with "... implementation, compliance and achievements of forest-related work under existing instruments ...".

The implementation of the IPF Proposals must be compatible with the implementation of other forest-related instruments. Since their endorsement at the 1997 UN General Assembly Special Session (UNGASS), it is beyond dispute that they reflect the present consensus on most international forest issues, and as such form the basis for any analysis concerning the present international forest regime. At the same time, the IPF Proposals have also to be seen as a part of the current international forest regime, which is composed by several legally binding and other non-binding instruments.

---

[1]   *See* IPF Programme Element V.1.

[2]   *See* IPF Programme Element V.2.

[3]   UN Doc. E/CN.17/1997/12.

However, the IPF Proposals provide little guidance in how they are to be related to other legal instruments, and only refer very generally to them; few IPF Proposals identify specific inter-linkages with existing instruments in political, strategic and operational terms. The point of departure for this paper, therefore, is how synergies can be achieved through implementation of the IPF Proposals.

2. Methodology

It is commonly assumed that effective "implementation" is the test of success for any international instrument, whether legally-binding or not. The paper will therefore begin with an examination of what "implementation" means in the context of the IPF and international treaties relevant to forests (Section II).

Section III will attempt to identify potential for synergies at the national level by surveying how forest-related Conventions can support the implementation of the main IPF Proposals. The paper will explore how far the Conventions are already being applied to forest-related matters, and how the implementation process would provide support to the countries' efforts to achieve sustainable forest management (SFM). Based on the findings in Section III, recommendations on how to further support coordinated national implementation of the these instruments are elaborated in Section IV.

Since it was beyond the scope of the paper to examine specific national cases, the findings and recommendations on how to enhance the implementation processes will be somewhat general in nature. Nonetheless, it is hoped that they might serve as a guide for further analytical work by countries regarding their specific national situation.

II. "Implementation" of Forest-related International Obligations

Most international obligations relevant to forests, either based on legally binding instruments or on "soft law", are ultimately aimed at the national level, "... recognizing that the most important part of work is action at the national level".[4] The development of international obligations that never ultimately reach the national level may be counterproductive in that they create the unfortunate illusion that the solution to a global problem is being pursued.

In addition, though, it will be seen below that implementation also has an international dimension. This is because international cooperation in some areas is needed to achieve the conservation, management and sustainable development of forests. Examples of these issues include international financial mechanisms and international trade in forest products.

1. The Implementation of the IPF Proposals

Implementing the IPF Proposals is high on the agendas of the IFF and other international organizations and institutions, as well as countries. Some examples of recent initiatives include: the national processes in Australia, Denmark, and the Netherlands, the "Inter-agency Partnership on Forests: Implementation of the IPF Proposals" by the Inter-agency Task Force on Forests

---

[4]   *See* Doc. IV/7.E. 8,   Fourth Meeting of the COP of the CBD.

(ITFF), FAO regional meetings in Asia, Africa and Latin America, and the Six-Country Initiative entitled "Putting the IPF Proposals into Practice".

The IPF Proposals suggest measures to be taken at international, regional and particularly national levels. However, it is not clearly spelled out in the IPF Proposals what ways and means countries should employ to translate them into action. The IPF Proposals are not self-executing; they neither contain precise obligations to be easily translated into the international context, nor set targets to be incorporated into national frameworks. Instead, they are designed so as to leave individual countries and/or organizations the discretion to determine how they will initiate the implementation. This is also because the IPF Proposals vary extensively in nature (basic principles, general guidelines and operational guidelines), and because the level of intervention is not always specified.

According to the results of the Six-Country Initiative,[5] which were later acknowledged by the IFF:

- The term "implementation" as used in the IFF Programme of Work means: (a) an assessment of the IPF Proposals, measured against the existing national forest-related frameworks in terms of relevance and value according to national priorities, constraints and ongoing activities as well as according to regional and international obligations; (b) the integration and internalization of the IPF Proposals into existing national processes; and (c) identification of country-specific measures to ensure that the IPF Proposals become part of the respective national processes, and is not an additional parallel exercise.

- The implementation mechanisms which were found to be useful in the national processes were those which are already in place to achieve sustainable forest management, such as forest sector reviews, forest and forest related policies and legislation, coordination mechanisms and various developmental and other programmes. Participation of all key stakeholder groups was seen as an important element of the implementation process. It was recognized that the implementation of the IPF Proposals requires nationally-established goals and objectives, which cannot always be directly derived from the IPF Proposals, but which should take into consideration objectives of other forest-related international instruments.

- Many of the IPF Proposals, particularly those under Programme Elements II to IV, do not suggest regulatory measures, or any concrete action to be undertaken at national level in order to comply with their objectives. Rather, such Proposals contain guidelines and principles, as well as fairly general directions to international organizations and other legal instruments. Implementation of these IPF Proposals certainly will have a different degree of practicability than those aiming directly at national level action.

2. The Implementation of Forest-related Conventions

Several existing international legally-binding instruments such as CBD, CCD, CITES, ITTA, FCCC et al. are relevant in implementing the IPF Proposals. These instruments address forest-related issues in specific contexts, embody the concept of sustainability, and address many cross-cutting issues relevant to forests. The latter include financial resources, technology transfer, trade and traditional knowledge, which are also contained in the Proposals. Indeed, the IPF underlined

---

[5] Report of the International Expert Consultation, June 29 to July 3, 1998 Baden-Baden, Germany.

the inter-linkages between the existing legal instruments and the implementation of the Proposals, and emphasized that

> "... existing legal instruments, financial and trade institutions and treaty bodies should mobilize their strengths and capacities in implementing the proposals for action ...".[6]

The implementation processes of these conventions are different from that of the IPF Proposals because of the different legal nature of the obligations. While the IPF Proposals constitute "soft law", imposing "only" political obligations upon the countries which have participated in the IPF, the conventions carry legally binding force. In most cases, this means that their obligations must be transposed into national legislation.

However, most modern international environmental treaties, especially those which play a most prominent role with regard to forests, CBD, FCCC, CCD, are framework agreements, containing overall goals and policies, rather than self-executing or detailed standards. Implementation of these "obligations of result" are determined by the individual parties. As such, the main decision-making is left to the national level, requiring parties to undertake a policy review process and establish national goals and objectives in line with the requirements of each convention. As alluded to above, these treaties contain provisions that are aimed at national action, as well as at international cooperation. Implementation, therefore has a different character, depending on whether it is at one or the other level.

One technique commonly employed by negotiators of framework conventions is to provide for implementing protocols or annexes. These protocols or annexes contain more precise obligations than in the convention itself, yet also carry legally binding force.

At the international level the conventions generally provide institutional mechanisms geared to steering and assisting the implementation of the convention. Conferences of the Parties, subsidiary bodies for scientific and technological issues, and the Secretariat, all have key roles to play in providing guidance on implementing the convention.

III. Review of the IPF Proposals and Links with Relevant Conventions

Prior to undertaking a review of the IPF Proposals and their links with relevant treaties, a few caveats must be mentioned. Firstly, there are numerous overlaps and inter-linkages between the IPF Proposals themselves. Secondly, there are many international mechanisms which are potentially relevant to the Proposals, although as mentioned above, many of these linkages are not specified in any detail. Thirdly, several important issues were not resolved by the IPF, for example those relating to international trade. Therefore, this analysis of the Proposals can only illustrate the diversity of relevant instruments and potential for linkages. Indeed, because it was not possible to be fully complete, only certain key Proposals are examined. They are presented below under the headings of their respective IPF Programme Elements.

---

[6]   Paragraph. 139, IPF Final Report.

1. IPF Programme Element I - Implementation of Forest Related Decisions of UNCED

1.1 Progress through National Forest and Land-Use Programmes

Under the Proposal set forth in Paragraph 17, the Panel encourages the countries to develop, implement, monitor and evaluate national forest programmes which include a wide range of approaches for sustainable forest management. Paragraph 17(a) is central, providing the structure for the implementation of most of the other country-level proposals. The description of the elements of NFP in Paragraph 17(a) combined with the related conclusions provides a summary of the present international consensus on the principles of an NFP. The implementation of this Proposal is under way in a number of countries which have begun initiating or revising their NFPs and other forest policy instruments. The Proposal notes that international agreements should be taken into consideration in the implementation process of NFP. Also, in its conclusions, the IPF stated that national forest programmes, as long-term iterative processes, should be – *inter alia* – consistent with international commitments. In this context further input from the Conference of the Parties to the CBD with respect to forest biological diversity is noted and welcomed.

Convention on Biological Diversity

The Convention on Biological Diversity (CBD) aims at the conservation of biological diversity, the sustainable use of its components and the fair and equitable sharing of the benefits arising from the utilization of genetic resources. It has been asserted by experts that the CBD's mandate is broad enough to encompass many of the issues of sustainable forest management. In the context of NFPs, as outlined in Paragraph 17, the most relevant provision is Article 6 of the Convention which requires parties to develop national strategies, plans, or programmes and policies for the conservation and sustainable use of biological diversity. It further requires parties to integrate these into relevant sectoral or cross-sectoral plans, programmes and policies. This Article reinforces Article 10(a), which requires the Parties to integrate the conservation and sustainable use of biological resources into national decision-making.

The implementation of these provisions at the national level will in most cases lead to the development of a national biodiversity strategy (NBS). Since biodiversity conservation and sustainable use of the components of biological diversity (e.g. forests) can only be effective through an integrative approach – in which the national programmes and policies of relevant sectors take into consideration biodiversity aspects – neither an NBS nor an NFP should be prepared and implemented in isolation from the other. Both the preparation and implementation of effective national biodiversity strategies and the development or revision of an NFP require a highly participatory process, in which different sectors and stakeholders have to be integrated. It is therefore beyond doubt that both these processes should be carried out in a coordinated and harmonized manner.

The potential synergies of the goals of the CBD and approaches for sustainable forest management as discussed under the IPF have clearly been recognized by the IPF and the meetings of the Conference of the Parties (COPs) of the CBD since 1995. The second COP (Jakarta 1995) dealt extensively with forests and biological diversity, and formulated a broad statement to the IPF stressing "the need to develop and implement methods for sustainable forest management which combine production goals, particularly those related to biological diversity." The third COP (Buenos Aires 1996) endorsed a background paper on biological diversity and forests emphasizing that the threefold objectives of the CBD can be applied to forests. With regard to IPF Programme Element 1.1, the Subsidiary Body on Scientific Technical and Technological Advice (SBSTTA) proposed to the third COP that additional inputs be sent to the IPF recommending that the NFP should be based on an ecosystem approach, which will integrate conservation measures and sustainable use of biological diversity into the NFP concept.

Although the aforementioned efforts to link the work under the CBD and the IPF at international level may have enriched both processes, no direct effect has yet been reported at the national level. However, the more recent documents prepared for the fourth meeting of the CBD Conference of the Parties (Bratislava 1998) indicate some political will to help foster better implementation of the CBD at the national level in conjunction with the IPF Proposals, in particular through the NFP process. COP IV notes that enhancing integration of the conservation and sustainable use of forest biological diversity into NFP and forest-management systems is an important task. It also reaffirmed that the IPF Proposals, in particular those related to national forest and land-use programmes, "provide a good basis for the implementation of key provisions of the CBD at the national level." This reflects an interesting approach towards implementation of the key provisions of the Convention; i.e. the COP does not expect a direct transformation process of its provisions into national policies, but seems to recognize the complementary character of the CBD with regard to forest issues. Indeed, the emphasis on a coordinated and harmonized approach to national implementation in relation to the IPF Proposals is appropriate.

Among the objectives of the Work Programme for Forest Biological Diversity, adopted by COP IV, national implementation appears to be a high priority.[7] Although the Work Programme underlines its focus "... on the research, co-operation and development of technologies, necessary for the conservation and sustainable use of forest biological diversity ..."[8] the elements of the Work Programme, in particular those which relate to Paragraph 17, emphasize action on the national level. Once the results of the case-studies and other exercises contemplated by the Work Programme have been produced and disseminated to Parties, improvement and enhancement of NFPs may arise.

UN Framework Convention on Climate Change (FCCC)

The relationship between the UN Framework Convention on Climate Change (FCCC) and approaches to sustainable forest management lies in the climate-related function of forests (i.e. as carbon sinks) and the effect of climate change on some forests. As regards the latter, the loss of certain forested areas is directly related to an intensification of the greenhouse effect in the atmosphere.

According to Article 4(1)(d), Parties commit themselves to "sustainable management", of forests, while Article 4(1)(c), calls for the promotion and cooperation of

> "practices and processes that control, reduce or prevent anthropogenic emissions of greenhouse gases ... in all relevant sectors, ... including forestry."

However, these articles have not yet materialized in concrete measures at national level. Although the second COP (Berlin 1996) underlined the importance of measures on forestry as integral components of a comprehensive national programme to address climate change, no measures which could directly support the implementation of Paragraph 17 have yet been launched.

The Kyoto Protocol to the FCCC, adopted by the third COP (Kyoto 1997) urges those Parties (Annex 1) which are committed to achieving its quantified emission limitation and reduction commitments, *inter alia* to promote "... sustainable forest management practices, afforestation and

---

[7] *See* Paragraph 3 of the Annex to Decision IV/7.

[8] Paragraph 1.

reforestation."[9] Article 3 (3) of the Kyoto Protocol allows for Annex I countries to meet their commitments through net changes in greenhouse gas emissions from sources and removals by sinks resulting from direct human-induced land-use change and forestry activities, limited to afforestation, reforestation and deforestation since 1990. Further clarification and decision-making on this issue is required before activities under the Kyoto Protocol could support the process of improving NFPs. In any event, this instrument is not yet in force.

Despite the apparent link between the FCCC and Paragraph 17 there are as yet no indications that the Convention is playing an important role in the implementation of Paragraph 17. However, it may be that synergy with regard to the FCCC could be achieved through the NFP process once it emerges that sustainable forest management practices help stabilize the greenhouse gas concentrations.

Desertification Convention (CCD)

The UN Convention to Combat Desertification in Countries Experiencing Serious Drought and/ or Desertification, Particularly in Africa (CCD) seeks to achieve its objectives by developing and implementing national action programmes to manage natural resources at the national and regional levels, particularly in the arid zones of Africa. The Convention relates to forests because forests perform important ecological functions that prevent desertification and arid conditions. In fact forest ecosystems help stabilize the soil, and hence deforestation fosters both desertification and land degradation.

Possible inter-linkages between Paragraph 17 and the implementation of the CCD are to be found in Article 4(2)(a), wherein the Convention advocates an integrated approach in planning, with respect to all physical, biological and socio-economic aspects of the process of desertification and drought. This would undoubtedly include national forest and land-use programmes. Thus it can be concluded that the CCD also covers themes of Paragraph 17 and therefore carries potential to achieve synergies.

Many Parties to the CCD are currently engaged, pursuant to Articles 9 and 10, in the preparation of their national action programme. It is recommended that "… the preparation of national action programmes shall be closely interlinked with other efforts to formulate national policies for sustainable development."[10] This would be an entry point to combine the processes of developing and/or reviewing NFPs and national action programmes under the CCD and thus improve the implementation of both.

Findings

The above analysis of the CBD, FCCC and CCD shows strong links, or even overlaps between the conventions and NFPs. The conventions as well as Paragraph 17 aim at the preparation and implementation of effective national strategies, plans, programmes which are of relevance to forests. These strategies, plans or programmes are the mechanisms through which the Parties of the Conventions or the IPF/IFF will organize and implement their approaches to sustainable use of forests or other components. This is a complex and multi-faceted task involving many sectors of government, as well as the private sector. The processes of developing these strategies, plans or programmes have to ensure that the various aspects of the different instruments all become part of the respective national policies, and that none of them is developed as an additional parallel

---

[9] Article 2(1)(a)(ii).

[10] Article 10.1.

exercise. The key seems to be a systematic, coordinated approach towards integrated implementation of all said elements into one coherent national policy for sustainable development.

1.2 Underlying Causes of Deforestation and Forest Degradation

The IPF Proposals with regard to the underlying causes of deforestation and forest degradation
(UC) aim primarily at research activities.[11] Thus, implementation of these Proposals for Action
is to be done in the context of on-going research projects on UC. Some of the IPF Proposals,
however, are more action-oriented and urge the countries to formulate and implement national
strategies for addressing UC and define policy goals for national forests.[12] These IPF Proposals
will require cross-sectoral action at national level, and a wide range of policies may need to be
reviewed. In this respect the IPF Proposals on UC are directly linked with Paragraph 17 on NFPs
and, therefore, the above comments on national implementation are equally applicable – e.g.
national strategies for addressing UC as well as the suggested reformulation of land policies and
legislation will need to become part of the NFP, and should not be regarded as an additional parallel
exercise.

Convention on Biological Diversity

The Panel encouraged countries in the context of UC to lend support to the preparation of the Work
Programme for forest biological diversity of the CBD.[13] The Work Programme of the Convention
on Biological Diversity (CBD), which has since been endorsed by the COP IV, does indeed address
UC issues. In particular, Element 2 aims to produce an analysis of human impacts on forest
ecosystems. One proposed outcome of Element 2 is an enhanced ability to prioritise research needs
and apply results, and an enhanced understanding of the role of traditional knowledge in ecosystem
management to minimize or mitigate negative influences, and to promote positive effects. The
Work Programme also proposes further research, particularly analysing measures for minimizing
or mitigating the underlying causes of forest biological diversity loss. In this context, the Work
Programme notes that it is essential that the CBD coordinate with IFF in order to enhance synergy
on these issues.

Desertification Convention

Because the socioeconomic causes of deforestation and desertification are similar – e.g. rural
poverty, ill-defined land use conversions, and rapid deterioration of forest resources through excess
logging and other unsustainable management practices – research activities under the CCD[14] may
be relevant to the implementation of the IPF Proposals on UC. Close coordination of activities of
both the CCD and IPF/IFF to obtain an enhanced understanding of negative human influences on
ecosystems, is recommended.

Findings

It is significant that the CBD and the IPF/IFF have already taken measures to ensure a coordinated
and harmonized approach in implementing the IPF Proposals relating to UC, particularly in

---

[11] Paragraphs 27 to 31.

[12] Paragraph 29(a).

[13] Paragraph 31(c).

[14] E.g. Article 17.

introducing coordination mechanisms for research projects. It can therefore be expected that synergies at national level will be achieved through a better understanding of UC. However, research on UC will only be made operational if policy feed-back at national level is materialized, such as the definition of appropriate policies and policy instruments, including institutional reforms. Key is to anchor the research results on UC into national policies, in particular into NFP and/or national biodiversity strategies.

1.3 Traditional Forest-related Knowledge (TFRK)

Most of the IPF Proposals under the heading of traditional forest-related knowledge are geared to the national level.[15] They are to be implemented by amending existing policies and legislation relating to intellectual property rights, regimes and frameworks for equity for traditional peoples, information management, capacity building, and research and training.

The IPF Proposals on TFRK are not to be considered as stand-alone provisions. Rather, they are expressly to be understood and implemented in the context of the Convention on Biological Diversity (CBD). The Panel explicitly recognized the mandate of the CBD in this context, and noted that the provisions of the CBD relevant to TFRK could cover the most important issues of TFRK.[16] The Panel also recognized the need to avoid duplication or overlap with other relevant intergovernmental processes.

Convention on Biological Diversity

The CBD has taken the lead in the international debate on TFRK and has established an *ad hoc* open-ended inter-sessional working group on TFRK at COP IV. The mandate of the working group includes providing advice on the application and development of legal and other appropriate forms of protection for TFRK, and providing the COP of the CBD with advice relating to the implementation of Article 8(j) and related provisions. In particular, it is to provide advice on the development and implementation of a programme of work at national and international levels.

The Work Programme for Forest Biological Diversity under the CBD recognizes the importance of TFRK in sustainable forest management.[17] In the context of Element 1, development of holistic and inter-sectoral ecosystem approaches, activities will be launched to further develop methodologies to advance the integration of traditional forest-related knowledge into sustainable forest management.

Desertification Convention

The Desertification Convention recognizes the value and relevance of traditional and local technology, knowledge, know-how and practices in several provisions.[18] It proposes that inventories of such knowledge and practices and their potential uses with the participation of local populations, be made and disseminated. The preparation of inventories and dissemination of information corresponds to IPF Paragraph 40(j), under which countries are encouraged to identify ways to inventory TFRK. The Committee on Science and Technology of the CCD invited the

---

[15] Paragraphs 40 (a) - (r).

[16] In particular Articles 8(j) and 10(c).

[17] Paragraph 3(d).

[18] E.g., Articles 18(2)(a) and 20(6).

parties to prepare such inventories. Exchange of experiences, in particular with regard to methodologies for information-sharing and disseminating inventories between the CCD and the IPF/IFF, may be mutually beneficial.

ILO Convention 169 on Indigenous and Tribal Peoples in Independent Countries

The implementation of the ILO Convention 169 could support the important role of indigenous peoples and forest-dependent peoples play in sustainable forest management, as recognized in IPF Paragraph 40. The Convention obligates Parties to introduce appropriate measures to protect and preserve the environment of the territories such people inhabit. Parties are urged to recognize the rights of ownership and property that the affected peoples possess to the lands they have traditionally inhabited.[19] These rights must include opportunities to participate in the utilization, management and conservation.

This Convention could therefore become relevant to the utilization of indigenous knowledge. However, given the fact that only few states have signed the Convention to date, it is unlikely that the Convention will do more than supplement the more widely ratified CBD, which is also far more specific with regard to TFRK. It is worth mentioning that the IPF Report itself does not refer to the Indigenous Peoples Convention in the context of TFRK. In sum, this Convention's relevance to supporting the implementation of Paragraph 40 can be expected to remain minor.

Findings

It is certain that the implementation of the IPF Proposals on TFRK will depend largely on the activities carried out under the CBD, in particular on decisions related to the implementation of Article 8 (j). The issue still needs to be clarified of what the potential could be of the relevant IPF Proposals in political, strategic or operational terms, and how they could be supportive to the implementation of Article 8 (j). In order to avoid overlaps and duplication, one option might be to transfer the mandate to implement the IPF Proposals with regard to TFRK in toto to the CBD and its bodies.

1.4 Fragile Ecosystems Affected by Desertification and Drought

The IPF Proposals 46 (a) to (f) urge countries and international organizations to undertake action to address the complex issues related to dryland forest ecosystems. Implementation of these IPF Proposals at national level would mainly be integrated with a country's NFP. Paragraph 46 (c) would result in the establishment of protected areas in drought-affected zones, in particular by creating the necessary legislative framework, survey mapping and gazetting of potential areas etc. These Proposals also call for strengthening and developing partnerships between stakeholders to promote sustainable management of ecosystems.

Desertification Convention

It is to be expected that the national implementation of Proposals 46, which are aimed at countries owning dryland forest ecosystems, will be closely coordinated with the activities under the Desertification Convention. Various passages of the Convention's Regional Implementation

---

[19] Article 14.

Annexes overlap with the proposals in Paragraph 46.[20] The Panel noted in Paragraph 46 (f) and (g) the link to the CCD and urged donors, international agencies and recipient Governments to develop efficient and coordinated programmes of international cooperation and action on forests and related ecosystems affected by desertification and drought. The Panel also invited the Committee on Science and Technology of the Conference of the Parties to the CCD to support research in this areas.

Findings

Although the context of the IPF Proposals on fragile ecosystems affected by desertification and drought and the CCD is fully recognized by the Panel, interestingly there is no mention of the need for national coordination of both. However, it has to be stressed that international cooperation programmes, as urged in Paragraph 46 (f), are too vague to guide any implementation. Such general provision is not sufficient in this respect but, as said before, mutual support in the implementation of both instruments will only be achieved by integrating them into national policies in a coordinated manner.

1.5 Impact of Airborne Pollution on Forests

Paragraph 50 is geared mainly to recommending approaches to be incorporated in national strategies for sustainable development for reducing damaging air pollution. The message of this Paragraph seems quite clear and is of particular importance for industrialized nations and economies in transition. Since the causes of airborne pollution lie outside the forest sector, and because of their wide impact on producers and consumers, dealing with these problems must be based on national dialogues between relevant stakeholders – i.e. government, industries and the general public.

Convention on Biological Diversity

Although the Convention on Biological Diversity does not directly refer to air pollution, implementation of Articles 7(c) and 8(l) could involve developing national strategies to reduce damaging air pollution. Article 7(c) requires the Parties to identify categories of activities which have or are likely to have significant adverse impacts on the conservation and sustainable use of biological diversity, and monitor their effects through sampling and other techniques ...

Pollution, in particular airborne pollution, is a well known threat to biological diversity. Article 8(l) obliges the Parties to "regulate or manage" the processes or categories of activities that have been identified under Article 7(c).

Findings

Implementation of this Proposal at the national level will involve a particular high degree of integrative approaches. How other global instruments might develop support for these national processes remains to be developed, although as outlined, the CBD offers some opportunity.

---

[20] E.g., the reference to "integrated and sustainable management of natural resources, including forests" in Article 3 (b)(i) of the Annex for Africa and Article 4 (c) in the Annex for Latin America/Caribbean.

1.6 Needs and Requirements of Developing and other Countries with Low Forest Cover

The Panel noted that while there are both developed and developing countries with low forest cover, the seriousness of problems encountered by these countries in satisfying their need for forest goods and services, which may have a very severe impact in developing countries. The IPF Proposals formulated in this subsection inter-link with other IPF Proposals, in particular with Paragraph 17 (NFP), Paragraph 50 (TFRK) and Proposals under Programme Element III, discussed below. The comments made in this paper with regard to the implementation of those Proposals are equally applicable to the IPF Proposals under Paragraph 58.

The IPF Proposals under this subsection are mostly geared to the maintenance and expansion of forest cover. Particular emphasis is placed on the initiation and implementation of plantation programmes. Countries are urged to embark on capacity-building programmes to promote participation and the use of TFRK. Another focus is on the development of adequate research information systems.

The Panel emphasized that the proposed measures under the present heading need to be coordinated with measures, *inter alia*, under the Convention on Biological Diversity, the United Nations Framework Convention on Climate Change, and the Desertification Convention.

Climate Change Convention

A clear link of the IPF Proposals under this subsection can be identified with the Kyoto Protocol under the FCCC, which proposes implementing and/or further elaborating policies and measures for the protection and enhancement of sinks and reservoirs of greenhouse gases. Article 3 of the Kyoto Protocol contains provisions with regard to future emission limitation and reduction commitments of industrialized countries, which may result in afforestation and reforestation measures in low forest cover countries.

Convention on Biological Diversity

Proposals 58b and 58v require that parties "establish or expand networks of protected areas." This relates to Article 8(a) of the CBD, which requires parties to "establish a system of protected areas..." and "develop ... guidelines for the establishment and management of protected areas ...". It also relates to the Work Programme for Forest Biodiversity of the CBD which aims, *inter alia*, to "identify the contribution of networks of protected areas to the conservation and sustainable use of forest biological diversity".[21]

Findings

As noted by the Panel, there are numerous measures under this subsection which need to be coordinated with measures under the existing UNCED Conventions. However, a coordinated approach and mutual support in implementing these measures at national level remains to be further explored.

---

[21] Paragraph 3(h).

2. IPF Programme Element II - International Cooperation in Financial Assistance and Technology Transfer[22]

Since the IPF Proposals under this subsection are aimed at international organizations, donors and recipient countries, their implementation will take place at both international and national levels. These actors are encouraged to find durable solutions by providing needed financial means for the management, conservation and sustainable development of all types of forest.

In the following the most relevant international financial mechanisms and international sources of finance for sustainable forestry are summarized.

During the IPF deliberations and in particular during the IPF Intersessional Workshop on "Financial Mechanisms and Sources of Finance for Sustainable Forestry" in South Africa (June 1996), it was emphasized the fact that existing financial resources are insufficient to achieve SFM on a global scale. The term "new and additional financial resources" was used in the IPF Report, making reference to the Rio Declaration on Environment and Development as well as the relevant parts of Agenda 21. Despite the fact that the content of the term remains controversial, the Panel concludes that none of the potential financial instruments, including domestic and international private sector investments, have mobilized innovative and new forms of finance. This is due to inadequate framework conditions such as (i) policies and legislation at the national and international level, as well as bilateral cooperation, (ii) country-specific social, economic, fiscal and ecological priorities, and (iii) in-country co-ordination involving broad stakeholder participation.

In order to strengthen international financial assistance, the Panel proposed:

(i)   the programming of ODA according to the needs of the developing countries,
(ii)   the creation of incentive systems and public and private partnerships,
(iii)   the devising and implementation of debt relief initiatives and
(iv)   consideration of the establishment of an international fund.[23]

With respect to increased private-sector investments, the Panel urged countries to set favourable legal and policy conditions, *inter alia*, concessional lending, guarantees and other incentives and appropriate market-based instruments. However, it is acknowledged that the absorptive capacity for both human and financial resources needs to be strengthened in most developing countries. Again in this subsection the Panel refers to NFPs as suitable coordination mechanisms.

According to Chapter 11 of Agenda 21, some US $ 31.25 billion annually is necessary to finance SFM up to the year 2000. This figure includes both contributions from domestic and international sources, with estimates a figure of US $ 5.67 billion or 18% coming from foreign private and public sources. Despite the fact that this figure is likely to be on the conservative side,[24] industrialized countries emphasize that it is only to be considered as a rough estimate that does not carry any legal obligations. Developing countries, however, tend to argue for using this figure, as well as for ODA to be in the order of 0.7 % of developed countries respective GNP.

---

[22]   This section will only consider the issue of financial assistance.

[23]   Paragraph 67.

[24]   Note by the Secretariat, Programme Element II.a: Matters left pending on the need for financial resources, UN Doc. E/CN.17/IFF/1998/7, 19 June 1998.

Thus, the amount of "new and additional financial resources" needed by developing countries to achieve sustainable development, not only in relation to forests, is still very much subject to global debate. A vast variety of financial instruments and mechanisms have been discussed since UNCED. Some of them have been legally established, others are still being debated or are under implementation in a pilot phase. Only the most relevant can be discussed here, particularly those linked to legally binding instruments.

Global Environment Facility

Paragraph 79 of the 1997 "Programme for the Further Implementation of Agenda 21" of UNGASS emphasized that the international community should explore "the flexibility of the existing mandate of the Global Environment Facility (GEF)". The GEF, established by the World Bank, UNEP and UNDP, provides financing to cover the incremental costs of measures designed to safeguard the global benefits of climate, biodiversity, international waters and the ozone layer. It has also been designated as the financial mechanism under the CBD and FCCC. Projects encompassing incremental costs are eligible for GEF funding in relation to land degradation, deforestation and desertification within the context of the GEF programme.

The limited mandate of the GEF and the restricted allocation of its financial resources (approx. US $ 3.4 billion since 1991) has led developing countries, in particular, to argue that the GEF's existence by no means excludes the establishment of other international global funds for SFM. The idea of such a global fund will likely be kept on the international agenda, even though most donor agencies and other international institutions regard the GEF as the most important environmental financial mechanism (if not the only one), especially in relation to the CBD and FCCC.

Framework Convention on Climate Change

The Kyoto Protocol under the FCCC establishes a Clean Development Mechanism (CDM) to assist the Parties of the Convention "in achieving compliance with their qualified emission limitation and reduction commitment". The role of the CDM is still very controversial, and the modalities as an incentive for the Annex I countries have not yet been clarified. With regard to the measures in developing countries under the Clean Development Mechanism, NGOs and many governments expressed their concern in Kyoto that accounting for reforestation projects with the CDM[25] creates an incentive to clear-cut in developing countries, if reforestation measures are financed without previous deforestation being accounted.

Some of these issues may be resolved after the pilot phase for the mechanism of Activities Implemented Jointly (AIJ) is completed in 2000. AIJ is presently being carried out in a manner that involves a variety of arrangements between the private sector and governments. The most outstanding achievements in this regard are the bilateral agreements concluded between the US, Norway and the Netherlands, respectively, with Costa Rica. Even though AIJ is promoted by the COP of the FCCC to serve as an effective tool in financial and operational terms, the concept has not been clearly defined under the FCCC. However, it is not yet clear whether AIJ projects will be eligible for crediting under the CDM. Notwithstanding the definitional and operational problems relating to AIJ and the CDM, this instrument has created great expectations with regard to financing SFM, especially with regard to securing private investments in the forestry sector.

---

[25]   Article 12.

Convention on Biological Diversity

In the context of CBD implementation, various financial arrangements have been tested involving domestic resources, the GEF, development banks, multilateral organizations and bilateral donors. However, within the COP, discussions have not yet produced very much. COP IV Decision IV/ 12 on additional financial resources requests the CBD Secretariat to prepare a report for COP V which will include proposals for:

a. monitoring financial support for the implementation of the Convention;
b. possible collaboration with international organizations, institutions, and relevant conventions and agreements;
c. exploring possibilities for additional financial support for the CBD programme of work (which includes forests);
d. examining the constraints to, opportunities for and implications of private sector support for the implementation of the Convention.

Desertification Convention

Unlike the UNCED Conventions, the CCD does not have a separate financial mechanism, even though the CCD Global Mechanism has been formally established. Its mandate is geared to the promotion, mobilization and rationalization of the transfer of financial and technological assistance to the countries of the South. The Parties of the CCD emphasized the necessity of in-country coordination and the increase of funds in line with structural conditions in the respective recipient countries. National action programmes and innovative partnership agreements are called for by the Convention to meet the needs of affected countries. This concept is very much in line with the trend in bilateral donor policies to promote national ownership of in-country coordination mechanisms.

Findings

The above summary on financial mechanisms and arrangements illustrates the diversity of instruments in place or under way to financially support effective implementation of the respective national forest programme at the country-level.[26] With regard to these mechanisms and instruments at international level, as well as innovative arrangements in finance particularly with the private sector, the effective support of national measures and programmes through Conventions such as CBD and FCCC will depend largely on the country-specific "mix" of instruments, according to the specific needs of local communities, NGOs and governments.

It is not likely that ODA overall will increase considerably over the next 10 years, despite the demands of some developing countries. This will require developing countries to revise their concept of public finance and will need to consider reliance on other sources of funds. Recent examples include debt-for-nature swaps, national environment funds and public-private partnerships that leverage mixed public-private financing. However, private sector investments in forestry will likely to be forthcoming only if there are predictable structural conditions, which entails reliable policies, good governance, accountability and participation of stakeholders and their institutions, including NGOs.

Further work is needed at the international level in order to clarify what is to be implemented and how. In addition to resolving some of the key controversies, the role of international instruments in promoting funding mechanisms also must be clarified. This may involve the further

---

[26] Paragraph 71(c).

development of international mechanisms, but will also need to focus on the development of innovative means which combine pubic and private sector financing from national and international sources.

3. IPF Programme Element III - Scientific Research, Forest Assessment and the Development of Criteria and Indicators for Sustainable Forest Management

Assessing the implementation the IPF Proposals under this Programme Element is not straightforward, since major overlaps with other IPF Programme Elements exist, particularly with "Progress through National Forest and Land-Use Programmes" (Ia), "International Cooperation in Financial Assistance" (II) and "Trade and Environment" (IV). In addition, the interface between the different issues within this IPF Programme Element calls for a holistic approach as between the various subsections.

3.1 Assessment of the Multiple Benefits of All Types of Forests

The assessment of forest resources aims to identify the various contributions of forests to national economies/societies.[27] Major obstacles to doing this include the lack of either national-level criteria and indicators (C&I),[28] or harmonization of forest assessments at international, regional, national and sub-national levels.[29] Data collection, monitoring and reporting should be executed according to agreed standards or C&I, even if done at different intervals.[30] FAO is called upon to continue with the preparations for the Global Forest Resource Assessment FRA 2000.[31] Support by other international processes or instruments is not mentioned by the Panel.

3.2 Forest Research

Forest research at the various levels needs to be prioritised and placed within an institutional network.[32] The Centre for International Forestry Research (CIFOR) is highlighted in the Proposals regarding to forest research.[33] As a member of the CGIAR group of institutions, CIFOR is mandated to: (i) play a coordinating and networking role in setting research priorities and in promoting research activities, and (ii) support country, regional and international research initiatives in the application of research results as identified. The UNCED Conventions, FCCC, CBD and CCD are called upon to support national and international research within their areas of competence and experience.[34] It can be concluded that implementation of these IPF Proposals needs to be performed in full cooperation with these conventions.

---

27   Paragraph 89(h).

28   Paragraph 89(a).

29   Paragraph 89(f).

30   Paragraph 89(g).

31   Paragraph 89(e).

32   Paragraph 94(a).

33   Paragraph 94(a).

34   Paragraph 94(b).

3.3 Methodologies for the Proper Valuation of the Multiple Benefits of Forests

Appropriate methodologies for the proper valuation of the multiple benefits of forests cannot be identified at any level without in-depth knowledge on the actual and potential contribution of forests to national economies/societies, and the current pattern of forest use. The Panel called for C&I to be identified at all levels so as to be able to judge proper values in monetary terms.[35] Translation of the relevant global, national and local values into monetary terms requires a detailed analysis of trade patterns, including current trade barriers and access to markets. It also includes quantification of the environmental and social costs resulting from underestimation of forest goods and services not included among the traditional forest products.

As a first step to tackle this important, but highly political topic, the Panel called for existing methodologies to be made use of so as to allow for more informed decision-making.[36] It also urged that further discussion on valuing the services provided by forests – including translating these values into monetary incentives for conservation and sustainable management – relating to biodiversity and climate change take place within the CBD and FCCC.[37] Not mentioned, though, are other international instruments and institutions such as CITES, ITTA and WTO, which would need to be involved in the deliberation of these issues, in order to achieve a more holistic result.

3.4 Criteria and Indicators for Sustainable Forest Management

For the criteria and indicators for sustainable forest management, the IPF Report provides an overview of the state of the international debate concerning criteria and indicators for sustainable forest management (C&I). The IPF does not itself resolve many of the ongoing questions. Indeed, the conclusions and IPF Proposals do not sufficiently distinguish between the quite different roles of C&I and their specific contexts such as policies, legislation or management plans at the different levels, e.g. international, national and management unit level.

Although the IPF asserts that the international debate should be continued, particularly with regard to divergent views on C&I at the global level,[38] the IPF Report only addresses itself to one international instrument – the CBD. It requests the COP to take note of the various ongoing C&I processes in forestry while defining the CBD biodiversity indicators.[39] A reference is made to the UNCED Forest Principles,[40] but, interestingly, not the DPCSD's indicators for sustainable development. The Panel urges countries to participate in international, regional and national processes on C&I, and to embark on a broad national and sub-national discussion on C&I with full participation of all interested parties, in order to prepare national-level C&I.[41]

---

[35] Paragraph 104(c).

[36] Paragraph 104(a).

[37] Paragraph 96.

[38] Paragraph 114.

[39] Paragraph 115(f).

[40] Paragraph 115(e).

[41] Paragraph 115(a) and (b).

4. IPF Programme Element IV - Trade and Environment in Relation to Forest Products and Services

The IPF Proposals under this subsection focus mainly on (i) market access, (ii) competitiveness of forest products, (iii) promotion of lesser used species, (iv) certification and labelling of SFM and forest products, (v) full cost internalization and (vi) market transparency.

The experience with the GATT and the World Trade Organization (WTO) has brought about a considerable reduction of the tariff barriers for many forest products. Further reductions are envisaged. However, concerns still exist in relation to non-tariff barriers. Official UN documents prepared for the IPF and IFF on this topic warn of new forms of "protectionism" and trade barriers deriving from environmental concerns.[42] However, the IPF itself took a slightly more positive view, in concluding that SFM should be promoted

> ... through mutually supportive trade and environmental policies in particular avoiding policies that have adverse impacts on the management, conservation and sustainable development of forests.[43]

However, given that there are numerous points of debate concerning on sustainable development, in general, and market liberalization, in particular, it would appear that a consensus on how to achieve this may not be very likely in the short term. Indeed, many of these issues are still being debated at the international level in other fora, and hence the conclusions and IPF Proposals in this subsection contain many matters left pending.

As mentioned, the Panel was concerned with the important theme of market access for forest products. The Panel was of the view that forest-related measures should not lead to disguised barriers to trade.[44] The issues in question which lead to perverse incentives and cause new barriers are: (i) domestic processing and production incentives, and (ii) environmental indicators and quantitative restrictions for imports. Paragraph 129 sets forth a so-called Proposal for Action, although in fact this paragraph only reports on discussions, for which there was no consensus, on options for an "... international agreement for forest products from all types of forests, based on non-discriminatory rules and multilaterally agreed procedures ..." such as WTO and the International Tropical Timber Agreement (ITTA). Considering the debate on a new legal instrument in global forestry under Category III of the IFF Programme of Work at this point in time, it seems most unlikely that the international community will proceed with the dialogue on a specialized international agreement to improve market access for forest products.

The Panel called upon relevant international organizations and national institutions to expand their work on market transparency for the trade in forest products and services – including possibly developing a global database – and to take measures to counter illegal trade in timber.[45] Competitiveness of forest products geared to the increase of productivity and efficiency in downstream processing,[46] as well as the promotion of lesser used species,[47] belong to this complex range of issues, but neither was treated in depth by the IPF.

---

[42] *See*, e.g. Report of the Secretary General on IPF Programme Element IIb, UN Doc. E/CN. 17/ 1998.

[43] Paragraph 116.

[44] Paragraph 128a.

[45] Paragraph 135(a) and (b).

[46] Paragraph 131.

[47] Paragraph 132.

As regards certification, the Panel, in Paragraph 133(a) urges countries

> ... to consider the potentially supportive relationship between sustainable forest manage-, ment, trade and voluntary certification and labelling schemes operating in accordance with relevant national legislation ...

In the Paragraphs that follow, 133(b)-(g), some qualifications to voluntary certification schemes are made, to avoid the danger of establishing new barriers, but at the same time recognizing their potential as promoters of sustainable forest management and improved market access.

The IPF Report, however, does not reconcile debates over the relationship between C&I and voluntary certification and labelling, but rather calls for further study.[48] The Report also lacks a detailed view on

(i) how to reach consensus on possible standards and procedures of voluntary certification, and

(ii) which institutions ought to be involved at the different levels, in particular at the international level to harmonize the ongoing efforts and to reach mutually supportive arrangements.

Category II(b) of the IFF's Programme of Work provides that the IFF should:

> ... consider the question of the relationship between obligations under international agreements and national measures, including measures imposed by sub-national jurisdictions recognizing that those matters are also considered in fora whose primary competence is to address trade issues ...

The latter point refers mainly to the mandates of the World Trade Organization (WTO) and the International Tropical Timber Organization (ITTO) and the measures taken which need to be carefully considered during the IFF process. However, due to the complexity of the issue of trade promotion through certification and labelling, it is clear that numerous organizations and institutions, e.g. the FCCC and the CBD, also need to be fully involved. The discussion and the measures taken on the promotion of trade and increased market shares cannot be limited to timber alone, but should certainly be expanded to trading forest benefits and services.

But, it is questionable whether the IFF can really carry out an in-depth dialogue on this complex issue. The recent Report of the Secretary General on trade and environment concludes that countries should use "... trade as an incentive for making the transition to sustainable forest management"[49] Its report calls upon WTO, FAO, ITTO, UNCTAD, EU and CIFOR to assist countries and the international community in increasing the availability of forest products and services from SFM and the market share of those products. But no mention was made of the Forest Stewardship Council (FSC) or the International Standard Organization (ISO), although both organizations are presently at the centre of the debate on certification and labelling.

Because the IPF Proposals reflect a lack of consensus on most substantive issues relating to trade, it is not yet possible to identify with precision how they relate to other forest-related international legal instruments. It is also not realistic to speak concretely about what "implementation" means in this context. This problem is compounded by the perception among some actors that conflicts exist between some multilateral environmental agreements and international trade

---

[48]   Paragraph 133(d)(ii).

[49]   UN Doc. E/CN.17/1998.

rules. Indeed, this perceived conflict is part of a larger policy agenda of achieving the objective stated in the IPF report of making trade and environment mutually supportive. As such, it may be that some trade-related issues relating to forests will only be resolved once a larger consensus on the relationship between trade and environment is reached.

IV. Recommendations on Supporting the Implementation of the IPF Proposals in the Light of Relevant International Legal Instruments

The findings in the previous sections reaffirm that there are numerous commonalties, linkages and even overlaps between the IPF Proposals and other relevant instruments. In particular, the UNCED Conventions and the IPF Proposals share an inherent relationship and mutual dependency which could produce synergy in the implementation processes of these instruments. However, such synergies do not yet play any substantial role. They are not yet sufficiently known to politicians and practitioners nor have they been made operational at country level.

The reasons for this are complex and diverse: (1) the results of the IPF were not conclusive on several key points, and therefore it is premature to speak about concrete implementation (2) the legal nature of the IPF Proposals, being soft law, restricts their relevance vis-à-vis the conventions (3) both the IPF Proposals as well as the relevant conventions are still at a very early stage of implementation (4) the potential for synergy in the implementation of these instruments has not been systematically explored.

Therefore, further activities involving additional actors and institutions at all levels are urgently needed in order to maximise complementarities and mobilise synergies of the instruments in question. Such action must take place at national as well as international levels. Thus, this final section seeks to draw out some recommendations for both levels with a view towards holistic and comprehensive sustainable forest management.

1. Towards a Coordinated and Harmonised Approach at the National Level

The conventions as well as the IPF Proposals for Action aim at the preparation of effective national strategies, plans or programmes towards sustainable forest management. These inter-linkages have been recognised to a certain extent by the Panel and the actors involved (COPs), although implementation activities at the national level do not fully reflect this. To improve the implementation of both, reduce the conflicts and overlaps, and produce synergy among them, a sharper focus on these "coordination issues" at national level is necessary. That should be done systematically under the framework of National Forest Programmes, which are internationally recognised as fundamental to achieving a holistic approach to sustainable development of all types of forests.

- The key national actors at the policy and planning level need to become knowledgeable on the overlaps and inter-linkages of the conventions and IPF Proposals.

- A process of assessment, interpretation and planning needs to take place to analyse the existing elements and instruments of the forestry and related sectors, to prepare for appropriate implementation of the international obligations. Part of this process could be the "mapping", as already recommended by the international community for the implementation of the IPF Proposals. The "mapping" of existing national components of a national forest programme and a "mapping" of the various forest-related international obligations could provide the framework for further systematic and coordinated implementation action.

- A high priority should be given to developing the institutions and capacities necessary to enable countries to translate the international obligations into action at national, regional, district and community levels.

- Coordination among the instruments in question must be nationally driven, with synergies formed to support national priorities. Coordination of implementation requires horizontal structures to support inter-ministerial consultation and cooperation, as well as to involve multi-stakeholder participation at all levels. Partnership approaches are recommended in this regard.

- Information and reporting systems which support the coordinated approach to implementation have to be explored and introduced at national level.

2. Elements to be Addressed at the International Level

Although the coordinated implementation of the IPF Proposals and related instruments is primarily a national task, much remains to be done at the international level to support it. This is particularly so for instruments and mechanisms in support of the IPF Programme Elements II to IV, since many issues involved have not yet been resolved and brought to a conclusion at international level. Measures and interventions at the international level to further enhance national-level implementation should include the following:

- Precise instructions by the COPs to their Secretariats or supporting bodies on how to work collaboratively with the secretariats of other conventions would foster potentials for national-level synergy.

- Shared reporting schedules and other ways to streamline reporting requirements could be developed between the instruments, thus lessening the reporting burden at national level.

- International cooperation to support sustainable forest management should be continued and improved, especially with through NFPs.

- More focused support for capacity building within the NFP process is required.

- There is a need to further develop the coordination of multilateral organizations by the Inter-agency Task Force on Forests (ITFF), especially in relation to their intermediary roles between international initiatives and national forest programmes.

- Attempts to coordinate and streamline global forestry research needs to be geared more towards national needs and priorities as identified in the NFP process.

- Issues related to finance, C&I, and trade require further international discussion to arrive at the stage where national action could be supported effectively.

The international community should define, within the IFF process (i.e. before 2000), appropriate means and institutional frameworks at the international level needed to secure the coordinated and synergetic implementation of the IPF Proposals and other relevant international instruments. Such a comprehensive and holistic approach to implementation is necessary to achieve sustainable forest management of all forests. At present, the fragmented nature of the present international forest regime means that this regime is not as effective in this regard as it might be. The IFF, in dealing with Category III, should consider the vital issues relating to coordination.

The Conservation and Sustainable Use of Forest Biological Diversity: The Role of the Convention on Biological Diversity

By Ruth Khalastchi and Ruth Mackenzie *

---

*   The authors would like to thank Ian Fry, Andrea Finger-Stich, Adam Delaney, Farhana Yamin, Kerstin Stendahl-Rechardt and Bill Jackson for providing information and comments on earlier drafts of this paper. Any errors or omissions are, of course, the responsibility of the authors.

I. Introduction

The Convention on Biological Diversity (CBD or the Convention)[1] is the first international treaty to address all aspects of biological diversity, including forests. The Convention was negotiated under the auspices of the United Nations Environment Programme (UNEP) in the light of a growing international recognition of and concern at the loss of the world's biological diversity, and a growing awareness of the economic value of that diversity. It was also negotiated against a backdrop of existing international and regional agreements which deal with various aspects of conservation and sustainable use. The Convention entered into force on 29 December 1993, and currently has 174 Parties.

The three-fold objectives of the Convention are the conservation of biological diversity, the sustainable use of its components, and the fair and equitable sharing of benefits arising out of the use of genetic resources (Article 1). The Convention takes a comprehensive, ecosystem approach to the conservation and sustainable use of biological diversity. It imposes few precise binding obligations upon Parties, but rather provides goals and guidelines. Most of the commitments of Parties are qualified and their implementation will depend upon the particular national circumstances and priorities of the individual Parties, and upon the resources made available.

It is widely recognised that forest ecosystems hold the vast majority of terrestrial biological diversity.[2] The conservation and sustainable management of forests is therefore crucial to the achievement of the objectives of the Convention.

1. Scope of Paper

The aim of this paper is to examine the role of the CBD in relation to forests. It focuses in particular on action under the Convention relevant to the conservation and sustainable use of forest biological diversity. The paper first outlines the provisions of the Convention which are of particular relevance to forests. It then considers the specific action on forest biological diversity currently being undertaken under the Convention. The paper then seeks to identify some of the factors which have affected the consideration of forest biological diversity under the Convention process. Finally, the prospects for future action on forests biological diversity under the Convention are considered.

Due to the specific context for which it has been prepared, this paper does not consider:

- the historical development of the international community's approach to forest issues; or

- arguments which have been advanced in relation to the elaboration of a protocol to the CBD on forests.

Clearly, any assessment of the role of the CBD in relation to forests needs to be viewed in the light of the background to, and the political dynamic which exists between, the various international institutional frameworks addressing forests-related issues.[3] These considerations are more specifically addressed in separate companion papers of this volume.

---

[1] Adopted in Rio de Janeiro, 5 June 1992, in force 29 December 1993; reprinted in 31 ILM (1992), 822.

[2] *See*, for example, the CBD Secretariat Note on the Draft Programme of Work for Forest Biological Diversity (UNEP/CBD/SBSTTA/3/5).

[3] *See* A. De Sa "*The Prospects for an International Environmental Agreement on Forests*", 10(1) International Environmental Affairs (1998) 18-39.

II. The CBD Framework: Relevant Provisions and Institutional Arrangements

Although the Convention does not specifically refer to forests, its entire scope is potentially of relevance as forests fall within the definition of the term "biological diversity"[4] in that they are both a component of, and a habitat for, terrestrial biological diversity. The Convention's provisions relate to the conservation and sustainable use of forest biological diversity and to the fair and equitable sharing of benefits arising from the use of forest genetic resources. It contains commitments regarding, *inter alia*, the establishment of protected areas and the development of incentives for the conservation of forest biological diversity.

This section outlines the provisions of the Convention which are of particular relevance to the conservation and sustainable management of forests.[5] The relevant institutional framework under the Convention is also briefly outlined. Section 3 below considers in more detail specific action initiated under the Convention of potential relevance to forest biological diversity.

1. The Provisions of the CBD of Particular Relevance to Forests

The Convention calls on Parties to conserve and sustainably use biological diversity by developing or adapting national strategies, plans and programmes and integrating the objectives of the Convention into relevant sectoral and cross-sectoral policies. It also requires Parties to integrate the conservation and sustainable use of biological diversity into national decision-making and adopt measures aimed at avoiding or minimising any adverse impacts on biological diversity.[6]

More specifically, the CBD imposes obligations in relation to both *in situ* conservation (in natural surroundings) and *ex situ* conservation (e.g. botanical gardens and gene banks), although the emphasis is primarily on the former. On *in situ* conservation, the Convention calls on Parties in particular to establish a system of protected areas or areas where special measures are required to conserve biological diversity and to promote the protection of ecosystems, natural habitats, and the maintenance of viable populations of species in natural surroundings. Parties are also called upon to rehabilitate or restore degraded ecosystems and prevent the introduction of, control or eradicate alien species which threaten ecosystems, habitats or species.[7]

The Convention leaves it to the Parties to identify the components of biological diversity important for conservation and sustainable use, in line with an indicative list of categories provided in an annex to the Convention. The list includes, *inter alia*, ecosystems and habitats with high

---

[4] Article 2 defines the term "biological diversity" for the purposes of the Convention as: the variability among living organisms from all sources including, inter alia, terrestrial, marine and other aquatic ecosystems and the ecological complexes of which they are a part; this includes diversity within species, between species and of ecosystems.

[5] *See* further Richard G. Tarasofsky, The International Forests Regime - Legal and Policy Issues, (IUCN, December 1995) and "The Global Regime for the Conservation and Sustainable Use of Forests: An Assessment of Progress to Date", 56(3) Heidelberg Journal of International Law (1996) 668-684.

[6] Articles 6 and 10(a).

[7] Article 8.

diversity, large number of endemic or threatened species, or wilderness.[8] Parties are also required to monitor important components of biological diversity, and to identify processes or activities likely to have adverse effects on biological diversity. As a first step to implementing Article 7, action on the development of indicators to monitor the status and trends of biological diversity is currently ongoing under the Convention (see section 3.4 below).

The Convention recognises that indigenous and local communities have a crucial role to play in the conservation of biological diversity, and acknowledges the significance of traditional knowledge and practices in the conservation and sustainable use of biological diversity. It calls on Parties to respect, preserve and maintain the knowledge, innovations and practices of indigenous and local communities and to protect and encourage the customary uses of biological resources in accordance with traditional customary practices compatible with the conservation and sustainable use of these resources.[9]

The Convention makes explicit reference to a number of additional policy and procedural measures to promote conservation and sustainable use. For example, it requires Parties to adopt economically and socially sound incentives for the conservation and sustainable use of biological diversity[10] and encourages research and training,[11] and public education and awareness.[12] With regards to procedures, Parties are obliged to introduce appropriate environmental impact assessment (EIA) requirements for projects likely to have a significant adverse effect on biological diversity.[13]

In line with the third stated objective of the Convention on access to genetic resources and the sharing of benefits resulting from the use thereof, Article 15 of the Convention reaffirms the sovereignty of Parties over their genetic resources, and recognises the authority of States to determine access to those resources. It requires that any such access be subject to that State's prior informed consent. The Convention also contains a number of provisions to ensure the fair and equitable sharing of benefits derived from the use of genetic resources. These provisions ultimately serve to encourage the conservation of biological diversity from which such resources are derived.

Lastly, the Convention contains provisions on access to and transfer of technologies[14] and on funding.[15] The Convention provides for the transfer of technologies relevant to the conservation and sustainable use of biological diversity, and technologies that make use of genetic resources to developing countries, taking into account existing patents and other intellectual property rights. It also provides for new and additional financial resources to be made available to enable developing countries to meet the "agreed full incremental costs" to them of implementing the obligations under the Convention. The Global Environment Facility (see section 2.2 below) has been designated to act as the financial mechanism of the Convention on an interim basis.[16]

---

[8] Article 7 and Annex I.

[9] Article 8(j) and 10(c).

[10] Article 11.

[11] Article 12.

[12] Article 13.

[13] Article 14.

[14] Article 16.

[15] Article 20.

[16] Article 39.

2. Institutional Arrangements

The governing body of the Convention is the Conference of the Parties (COP), which has met four times to date. The last meeting took place from 4 to 15 May 1998, in Bratislava, Slovakia. The next COP will take place in the second quarter of the year 2000.[17] The scope of the Convention has meant that over the last four years the COP has been required to deal with a heavy agenda. The COP has initiated work in a number of areas to elaborate and clarify aspects of the Convention, and has taken numerous procedural and substantive decisions.[18]

At its first meeting in 1994, the COP adopted a medium-term programme of work for the years 1995-1997, and suggested that focused work programmes should be developed for specific issues. The first work programmes to be developed have been on marine and coastal biological diversity and agricultural biological diversity. The medium-term programme of work also included consideration of a future work programme for terrestrial biological diversity[19] which has eventually led to the development of a work programme on forest biological diversity (see section 3.2 below). The COP continues to focus on particular ecosystems at each of its ordinary meetings. At its last meeting in May 1998, the COP focused on inland water ecosystems. It also considered its longer-term programme of work and outlined its thematic focus for the next three COPs. Forests will be a particular focus of the sixth meeting of the COP,[20] which will most likely be held in the year 2002.[21]

The Convention establishes two institutions to provide the COP with assistance in carrying out its work. A Subsidiary Body on Scientific, Technical and Technological Advice (SBSTTA) has been established to provide the COP with advice and recommendations on scientific, technical and technological aspects of the implementation of the Convention. SBSTTA is open to all Parties to the Convention, and has so far met annually in advance of the COP.[22] Administrative support to both the COP, SBSTTA and other Convention bodies[23] is provided by the Secretariat, located in Montreal, Canada.

The financial mechanism,[24] operated by the Global Environment Facility (GEF), is also a key component of the Convention's institutional structure. The GEF was established in 1991 as a joint initiative of the UNEP, UNDP and the World Bank. The financial mechanism functions under the authority and guidance of, and is accountable to, the COP. The first meeting of the COP adopted guidance to the financial mechanism, which is kept under review at each COP meeting. GEF resources are available for projects and activities in four focal areas, one of which is Biological Diversity, which includes an Operational Programme on forest ecosystems (see further section 3.3 below).

---

[17] Decision IV/16.

[18] 82 decisions have been taken by the COP over a period of four years.

[19] UNEP/CBD/COP/1/17 - Report of the First Meeting of the Conference of the Parties to the Convention on Biological Diversity; Decision I/9.

[20] Decision IV/16.

[21] Although the last four COPs have been held on an annual basis, COP 4 decided that the next meeting of the COP will not be until the year 2000. It is likely that future COPs will be held on a biannual basis.

[22] Article 25, CBD. To date SBSTTA has met on three occasions (4-8 Sept 1995; 2-6 Sept 1996; 1-4 Sept 1997).

[23] Decision II/5 established an open-ended *ad hoc* working group to negotiate a protocol on biosafety.

[24] Article 21, CBD.

III. CBD Action to Date on Forests

To date, specific action undertaken in relation to forest biological diversity under the Convention falls into three categories: (i) input from the CBD into the Intergovernmental Panel on Forests (IPF) and the Intergovernmental Forum on Forests (IFF) processes; (ii) elaboration of a focused work programme on forest biological diversity; and (iii) guidance to the GEF. Other activities currently being undertaken under the CBD, while not specifically focusing on forest biological diversity, are potentially of relevance to forest biological diversity.

This section considers these activities in turn. It will be shown that the discussions and actions which have taken place within the context of the work of the IPF/IFF have had a direct influence on the discussions that have taken place within the context of the CBD, and the progress that has been made to date in relation to forest biological diversity. The existence of two international political fora dealing with forests has somewhat served to hamper progress under the Convention as much time has been spent on debating the suitable forum to address matters relevant to forest conservation and sustainable management, and on working towards complementarity and synergy rather than concrete action. This is most apparent in relation to the development of the forests work programme under the CBD considered in section 3.2 below.

1. Input into the IPF/IFF Process

The third session of the Commission on Sustainable Development (CSD) established an open-ended *Ad Hoc* Inter-Governmental Panel on Forests (IPF) to follow-up work on forests.[25] The Panel's mandate was to pursue consensus and formulate options for further actions to support the management, conservation and sustainable development of forests.[26]

The IPF provided its final conclusions and proposals for future action to the CSD for transmission to the UN General Assembly Special Session (UNGASS) in 1997. UNGASS approved the IPF proposals for action and decided to continue the dialogue on forests within the open-ended *Ad Hoc* Intergovernmental Forum on Forests.[27] UNGASS also called, *inter alia*, for international organisations to implement the IPF proposals for action through enhanced inter-agency and institutional coordination, (including by means of the Inter-agency Task Force on Forests (ITFF)), cooperation (involving financial resources, capacity-building, research and the transfer of technology) and effective partnership with major groups in particular indigenous and local communities.

---

[25] At the United Nations Conference on Environment and Development (UNCED) in 1992, efforts to conclude a legally binding instrument on forests were unsuccessful. Instead the Non-Legally Binding Authoritative Statement of Principles for a Global Consensus on the Management, Conservation and Sustainable Development of all Types of Forests (the Forests Principles) was adopted. At its 1995 session the CSD was required to review progress on "combating deforestation" and the management, conservation and sustainable development of forests as dealt with in Agenda 21, Chapter 11, and the Forests Principles.

[26] *See* Report of the *Ad Hoc* Intergovernmental Panel on Forests on its Fourth Session, New York, 11-21 February 1997, (E/CN.17/1997/12).

[27] The role of the IFF is to facilitate the implementation of the IPF proposals for action; review, monitor and report progress in the management, conservation and sustainable development of all types of forests; and consider matters on which consensus was not reached under the IPF (trade, transfer of technology and financial resources); *see* report of the IFF at its first session, New York, 1-3 October 1997 (E/CN.17/IFF/1997/4).

The IPF conclusions and proposals for action contain a number of references to the CBD, and the Convention itself has had some involvement in the IPF process. In November 1995, the second meeting of the COP adopted a statement from the Convention to the IPF on biological diversity and forests.[28] The COP noted the crucial role of forests in maintaining global biological diversity and called for a dialogue with the IPF on issues related to forest and biological diversity. The COP further noted that *in situ* forest conservation activities, including the establishment and management of protected areas, have an important role to play in the achievement of biological goals for sustainable development forest management, and should be integrated in national forest and land-use plans.[29] The IPF recommendations on traditional forest-related knowledge (TFRK) were formulated with input from the CBD Secretariat and the Parties to the CBD. In response to an invitation by the Inter-agency Task Force of the IPF, the COP, at its second meeting in 1995, requested the Secretariat to provide advice and information pertaining to the relationship between indigenous and local communities and forests. The documents prepared by the Secretariat would contribute to the preparation of the Report of the Secretary-General on "Traditional forest-related knowledge" to be considered by the IPF, under Programme element 1.3 of its programme of work.[30] The IPF proposals for action, *inter alia*, call for the promotion of "activities aimed at advancing international understanding of the role of TFRK in the management, conservation and sustainable development of all types of forests to complement activities undertaken by the Convention".[31] The CBD is to continue to take the lead on promoting further understanding on how TFRK might contribute to sustainable forest management.

In September 1996, the second meeting of the CBD's SBSTTA recommended that the following inputs from the CBD be transmitted to the IPF:[32]

- biological diversity considerations should be integrated fully into the IPF recommendations and proposals for action. IPF should also consider ways to deal with identified gaps in forest biological diversity knowledge;

- in relation to programme element I.1 of the IPF on national forest and land use plans, strategies for sustainable forest management should be based on an ecosystem approach, which will integrate conservation measures (e.g. protected areas) and sustainable use of biological diversity. Methodologies need to be developed to assist countries in identifying sites of high interest for biological diversity. These recommendations should take into account national financial circumstances, laws and regulations.

- in relation to the programme element of the IPF dealing with criteria and indicators, conservation of biological diversity and the sustainable use of its components, as well as

---

[28] Decision II/9, Annex.

[29] Decision II/9, Annex, paragraph 13.

[30] *See* document UNEP/CBD/SBSTTA/2/Inf.3. In consultation with the IPF Secretariat, the CBD Secretariat prepared a note on "Traditional forest-related knowledge" (E/CN.17/IPF/9) for the initial discussion of this programme element at the second session of the Panel. The document was further elaborated for the Panel's third session in accordance with the guidance provided by the Panel at its second session and taking into account views of governments, organisations and individual experts.

[31] To facilitate an effective and coordinated response for the implementation of those IPF proposals for action directed at international organisations, the Inter-agency Task Force on Forests (ITFF) has prepared an implementation plan, entitled "Inter-agency Partnership on Forests: Implementation of the IPF Proposals for Action by the ITFF". The CBD Secretariat is a member of the ITFF and the lead agency for Programme element I.3 on "Traditional Forest-related Knowledge".

[32] Recommendation II/8.

the maintenance of forest quality, as part of sustainable forest management, should be substantively included in the deliberations of the IPF.

These recommendations are generally reflected in the IPF proposals for action, which, in particular, call for national forest programmes to take into account "ecosystem approaches that integrate the conservation of biological diversity and the sustainable use of biological resources."[33]

The IPF proposals for action contain a number of other references to the CBD, including on:

- underlying causes of deforestation and forest degradation: Parties should support the preparation of the programme of work for forest biological diversity with respect to analysing measures for mitigating the underlying causes of biological diversity loss;[34]

- needs of countries with low forest cover: such countries should establish or expand networks of protected areas, buffer zones and ecological corridors to conserve biological diversity, particularly in unique types of forests;[35]

- forest research: the CBD should promote research and analysis and address gaps in existing knowledge;[36]

- criteria and indicators: the CBD should take note of the various existing initiatives on criteria and indicators to ensure that the work done by it on biological diversity indicators would be consistent with and complementary to them.[37]

Moreover, the IPF noted the need for collaboration on various cross-cutting issues, including strengthening cooperation and technology transfer and the development of methodologies for valuing forest biological diversity.

Similarly, the CBD has noted in relation to its work on forests biological diversity (see below) the need to effectively coordinate and complement rather than duplicate work being undertaken under the auspices of the IPF/IFF.

2. Work Programme on Forest Biological Diversity under the CBD

The origins of the existing programme of work on forest biological diversity lie with the recommendations and priorities elaborated at the second meeting of SBSTTA in September 1996 (SBSTTA 2). Forest biological diversity was considered by SBSTTA 2 under its agenda item on terrestrial biological diversity in preparation for the third meeting of the COP, which was to consider its future programme of work for terrestrial biological diversity in the light of the outcome of deliberations of the third session of the CSD.

In May 1998 at its fourth meeting, the COP adopted the work programme for forest biological diversity.[38] The work programme is based largely on the recommendations of SBSTTA as adopted

---

[33] IPF Proposals for Action, paragraph 17(a).

[34] IPF Programme Element I.2.

[35] IPF Programme Element I.6.

[36] IPF Programme Element III.2.

[37] IPF Programme Element III.3.

[38] Decision IV/7.

at its third meeting in September 1997. It is divided into three phases, each of three year duration, although the COP noted that the time-frame needed to remain flexible in the light of the Convention's longer-term programme of work and the work being undertaken by the IFF. It is subject to periodic review and interim reports are due after each three year phase to assess implementation.

In many ways, the programme of work as adopted at COP 4 reflects the underlying political dynamic amongst the Parties to the CBD and the contentious discussions in the negotiations on this issue, resulting in a programme of work, which, at least in the initial stages, focuses more on the gathering of information, institutional cooperation and collaboration, and the identification of further research priorities than on concrete substantive output-orientated activities. Moreover, the emphasis on coordination and avoiding duplication of work, and in particular the reference to waiting for IFF's consideration of certain common priorities, suggests an emphasis on synergy, and, to some extent, subordination of the CBD's work on forest biological diversity to that of the work of the IFF.

The objectives of the work programme are stated to be as follows:

- to encourage and assist Parties to develop measures for enhancing the integration of conservation and sustainable use of biological diversity into their national forest and land-use programmes and forest-management systems;

- to facilitate the implementation of the objectives of the Convention based on the ecosystem approach;

- to provide an effective and complementary tool to national forest and land-use programmes for the implementation of the Convention at the national level;

- to identify traditional forest systems of conservation and sustainable development use of forest biological diversity and to promote the wider application, use and role of traditional forest-related knowledge in sustainable forest management and the equitable sharing of benefits, in accordance with Article 8(j) and other related provisions of the Convention;

- to identify mechanisms that facilitate the financing of relevant activities;

- to contribute to ongoing work in other international processes, in particular to the implementation of the IPF's proposal for action and the work of the IFF;

- to contribute to the access to and transfer of technology; and

- to identify the contribution of networks of protected areas to the conservation and sustainable use of forest biological diversity.

As a first step towards achieving these objectives, COP 4 outlined the work to be undertaken in the initial phase of the work programme. The elements of the work programme (based largely on the recommendations of SBSTTA 3) involve:

- synthesising existing knowledge of holistic and intersectoral ecosystem approaches that enhance the integration of forest biological diversity conservation into sustainable forest management;

- analysing the ways in which human activities, in particular forest-management practices, influence biological diversity and assessing the ways to minimise or mitigate negative influences and promote positive influences;

- developing methodologies to advance the elaboration and implementation of criteria and indicators for forest biological diversity.

In respect of each of these programme elements, the focus of the initial phase is primarily on research, institutional cooperation and collaboration, and the identification of further priority research areas. The activities outlined in the work programme, *inter alia*, involve examining existing methodologies, undertaking case-studies, sharing information, developing the means and mechanisms to improve the identification and prioritisation of research activities and the dissemination of research results, and assessing existing initiatives.

COP 4 also suggested a variety of mechanisms to achieve the work identified, including through the use of workshops, liaison groups, networks of experts, the clearing-house mechanism, data and meta-databases and remote sensing technologies, national pilot projects, as well as through cooperation and collaboration with the ITFF, the IFF and national institutions and other relevant bodies. Emphasis is also placed on collaborative efforts with other international processes in particular with the Desertification Convention and the Climate Change Convention.

Absent from the work programme however is an agreed institutional framework and a specific timetable for achieving the outputs identified. Rather, the emphasis is on flexibility. COP 4 stressed that the work programme should be "flexible enough to reflect and respond to changing conditions, including but not limited to, the outcome of and the priorities to be identified by the IFF".

Moreover, the role of the Secretariat is unclear. Other than a request to compile a synthesised report on information on forest biological diversity made available from Parties particularly in their national reports, the work programme does not allocate particular tasks to the Secretariat. Although a Programme Officer on terrestrial biological diversity is now in place in the Secretariat, this post also has responsibility for work on terrestrial ecosystems other than forests, including drylands and grasslands which will form the ecosystem focus of COP 5. It is not yet clear therefore what staff resources will be dedicated to the forests work programme.

In addition, while there was much discussion at COP 4 on the establishment of an *ad hoc* technical expert group on forests, the lack of agreement to establish such a group means that implementation of the work programme falls largely on SBSTTA. SBSTTA might, however, choose to establish such an expert group to progress work on forests under the CBD in the future (see section 5 below).

In addition to the programme elements listed above, COP 4 noted the further research and technological priorities which had been identified by SBSTTA 2 (Recommendation II/8 – see below) and that other issues are likely to be identified in the review and planning process of the work programme. The COP considered that these were important issues that had been "brought forward into the Convention from the IPF proposals for action", that these issues would be discussed by the IFF at its scheduled meetings in 1998 and 1999 and that it was "essential that the Convention on Biological Diversity coordinates with IFF in order to enhance synergy on these issues as they intersect the programme of work for forests under the Convention". The COP thus determined that "following input from IFF on these priorities, the Conference of the Parties may wish to consider incorporating them in phases 2 and 3 of the work programme".

COP 4 did however single out two of the research priorities: on analysing the measures for minimising or mitigating the underlying causes of forest biological diversity loss, and on integrating protected areas in the ecosystem approach to sustainable forest management. While the COP did not provide for any specific actions and outputs in relation to these priorities, their reintroduction by the COP marked a positive step (SBSTTA 3 had included them in the additional research priorities to be considered as future work is developed – see below section 3.2.2.1).

An assessment of the background to the elaboration of the work programme serves to illustrate the current approach by the Parties to the CBD on forest biological diversity. It signals a weakening and delaying of concrete action under the Convention and a "wait and see" approach, reflective of the contentious nature of the issue and the fact that forests are being considered in other relevant international fora.

2.1 Elaboration of the Forest Biological Diversity Work Programme

The first meeting of the Conference of the Parties[39] (COP 1) requested SBSTTA to consider the ways and means in which the COP could start the process of considering the components of biological diversity particularly those under threat, and to identify the action which could be taken under the Convention. At its first meeting in September 1995, SBSTTA noted, *inter alia*, the establishment of the IPF and, recognising the importance of forests for the conservation and sustainable use of biological diversity, recommended that the COP consider whether an input into the IPF process would be desirable (Recommendation I/3). SBSTTA 1 further suggested that the following main elements be considered:

- identification of the main causes that lead to the decline of forest biological diversity, and development and promotion of the use of methods for the management, conservation and sustainable use of forests;

- development and application of the ways and means to ensure fair and equitable sharing of benefits derived from the use of forest genetic resources as an incentive to maintain forest biological diversity;

- promotion of the protection of the knowledge, innovations and practices of indigenous and local communities embodying traditional lifestyles, and compensation through the equitable sharing of the benefits arising from the use of such knowledge, innovations and practices, in accordance with Article 8(j) of the Convention on Biological Diversity, in order to improve conservation and sustainable use of forest biological diversity.[40]

As noted above, COP 2 adopted a statement from the Convention to the IPF on biological diversity and forests. It also requested the CBD Secretariat to produce a background document on the links between forests and biological diversity, in order to consider, at COP 3 whether further input into the IPF process was required.[41] The background document[42] was reviewed by the SBSTTA at its second meeting in September 1996.

SBSTTA 2 identified the following research and technological priorities:

- building the scientific foundation and methodologies necessary to advance the elaboration and implementation of criteria and indicators for forest quality and biological diversity conservation as part of sustainable forest management;

- analysing the role of biological diversity in forest ecosystem functioning;

- analysing measures for mitigating the underlying causes of biological diversity loss;

---

[39] Decision I/8 on Preparation of the participation of the Convention on Biological Diversity in the third session of the Commission on Sustainable Development; *see* Report of the First Meeting on the Conference of the Parties to the Convention on Biological Diversity; (UNEP/CBD/COP/1/17).

[40] Recommendation I/3.

[41] Decision II/9, paragraph 2(b).

[42] UNEP/CBD/SBSTTA/2/11.

- advancing scientific and technical approaches to a) rehabilitating degraded and deforested ecosystems and b) enriching biological diversity in forest plantations;

- identifying gaps in knowledge in the areas of fragmentation and population viability, to include mitigation options such as corridors and buffer zones;

- assessing ecological landscape models, the integration of protected areas in the ecosystem approach to sustainable forest management and the representativeness and adequacy of protected areas networks;

- analysing scientifically the ways in which human activities, in particular forest management practices, influence biological diversity and assessing ways to minimise or mitigate negative influences;

- developing assessment and valuation methodologies for the multiple benefits derived from forest biological diversity.

At its third meeting the COP endorsed the recommendations of SBSTTA 2, and requested the Secretariat to take account of the research and technical priorities listed above in exploring ways and means to cooperate with the IPF, or any successor, "with a view to developing common priorities for further consideration". The COP further requested the Secretariat to develop a focused work programme for forest biological diversity, on the basis that the work programme should:

- initially focus on research, cooperation and the development of technologies necessary for the conservation and sustainable use of forest biological diversity;

- take account of the outcome of the IPF and forest-related fora;

- facilitate the application and integration of the objectives of the CBD in the sustainable management of forests at the national, regional and global levels, in accordance with the ecosystem approach;

- complement and not duplicate the work of relevant international fora, notably the IPF;

- complement existing national, regional or international criteria and indicator frameworks for sustainable forest management; and

- incorporate traditional systems of forest biological diversity conservation.

The Secretariat was requested to work closely with IPF and other relevant institutions. Parties to the Convention were encouraged to assist with the development of the work programme.[43]

COP 3 had requested SBSTTA to advise on the draft work programme and report back to it at its fourth meeting in May 1998. COP 3 also requested SBSTTA, in the light of the work programme and the research and technical priorities it had identified,[44] to advance its scientific, technical and technological consideration of forest biological diversity by initially focusing on the following:

- methodologies necessary to advance the elaboration and implementation of criteria and indicators for the conservation of biological diversity as part of sustainable forest management;

---

[43] Decision III/12, paragraph 7.

[44] Recommendation II/8.

- scientific analysis of the ways in which human activities, in particular forest management practices, influence biological diversity and assessment of ways to minimise or mitigate negative influences.

2.1.1   The Helsinki Liaison Group

In line with Decision III/12, paragraph 7, which called on all Parties to assist the Secretariat in the preparation of the work programme, the Secretariat established a roster of experts on forest biological diversity. The Secretariat convened a meeting of a liaison group on forest biological diversity, the participants of which were drawn from the roster, held in Helsinki from 25 to 28 May 1997, on the invitation of the Government of Finland. The mandate of the liaison group was to identify priority elements for a work programme on forest biological diversity under the Convention.

The liaison group identified a number of potential elements for a work programme, and sought to recommend how these might be addressed. The group considered that the ecosystem approach to managing forests and the requirement under Article 6(b) to integrate the conservation and sustainable use of biological diversity into relevant sectoral and cross-sectoral plans, programmes and policies were the two most important features of the CBD in terms of addressing forest-related issues. It also considered that the "value added" of a forest work programme could be to analyse and develop scientific, technical and technological advice useful to all CBD Parties on how to actually operationalize the ecosystem approach and Article 6(b).

The liaison group developed a five-step framework for addressing the potential elements, which centred on the ecosystem approach and the implementation of Article 6(b). The framework not only identified the relevant steps but detailed a host of possible outputs, which included, *inter alia*, definitions; guidelines; principles; legislative, institutional, economic and incentive measures; policy reform, training and awareness raising activities; and identification of research needs and priorities.

2.1.2   The Draft Work Programme on Forest Biological Diversity

On the basis of the recommendations of the liaison group and input from the IPF Secretariat and other relevant institutions, the CBD Secretariat proposed a draft programme of work on forest biological diversity based on the following five programme elements:

- defining the ecosystem approach to forest biological diversity;

- identifying the conditions for implementing Article 6(b) of the Convention (integration of forest biological diversity considerations into relevant sectoral and cross-sectoral planning);

- formulating and implementing criteria and indicators of forest biological diversity;

- identifying research and information needs and mechanisms;

- identifying best practices and approaches in relation to forest biological diversity.

In addition, the Secretariat proposed that the consideration of traditional systems of conservation and sustainable use of forest biological diversity and the wider application of such knowledge in accordance with Article 8(j) and other related provisions of the Convention should be included as an integral component of each of these elements.

The draft programme of work sought to take into account and complement rather than duplicate work undertaken under the auspices of the IPF and other forest-related fora. For each programme element, the draft set out the ways and means, the outputs and the costs of achieving the work identified.[45]

2.1.3 Consideration of the Draft Programme of Work on Forest Biological Diversity by SBSTTA 3

As mentioned above, SBSTTA was requested to advise on the draft programme of work for forest biological diversity and to report to COP 4. At its third meeting in September 1997, SBSTTA recommended that the programme of work on forest biological diversity should focus on "research, cooperation and technology development" in respect of the following priority areas:

- holistic and intersectoral ecosystem approaches that integrate the conservation and sustainable use of biological diversity as well as socio-economic considerations;

- scientific analysis of the ways in which human activities, in particular forest management practices, influence biological diversity;

- assessment of the ways to minimise or mitigate negative influences;

- methodologies necessary to advance the elaboration and implementation of criteria and indicators.

SBSTTA 3 also recommended that the "remaining research and technological priorities identified in SBSTTA Recommendation II/8",[46] be taken into consideration as future work is developed.

According to SBSTTA 3, the programme of work should, *inter alia*, reflect a rolling three-year planning horizon (subject to periodic review by the SBSTTA); that the activities identified in the work programme be demand-oriented and selected according to the interests of countries; that care is taken to minimise duplication of work with similar ongoing activities in other fora and that the activities identified be consistent with the proposals for action of the IPF and in close cooperation with the IFF and other related fora. Significantly, SBSTTA 3 also recommended to the COP "that it recommend that Parties and countries and international funding institutions, including GEF, give priority to the allocation of resources to aid progress towards achieving the objective of the Convention with regard to forest biological diversity".[47]

---

[45] UNEP/CBD/SBSTTA/3/5.

[46] The research and technical priorities identified in SBSTTA Recommendation II/8 falling under this category are: analysing the role of biological diversity in ecosystem functioning; analysing measures for mitigating the underlying causes of biological diversity loss; advancing scientific and technical approaches to (a) rehabilitating degraded and deforested ecosystems and (b) enriching biological diversity in forest plantations; identifying gaps in knowledge in the areas of fragmentation and population viability, to include mitigation options such as corridors and buffer zones; assessing ecological landscape models, the integration of protected areas in the ecosystem approach to sustainable management and the representativeness and adequacy of protected areas networks; and developing assessment and evaluation methodologies for the multiple benefits derived from forest biological diversity.

[47] Recommendation III/3.

The recommendations of SBSTTA on the draft work programme reflect in many ways the lack of consensus and tensions which exists among the Parties to the Convention on this issue. In particular, SBSTTA 3's recommendation seems to have lost many of the suggestions for substantive output-oriented work put forward by the Helsinki liaison group. For example, the liaison group had recommended that work be undertaken in relation to the identification of best practices and approaches in relation to forest biological diversity. The liaison group and COP 3 had also recommended that the programme of work should "incorporate traditional systems of forest biological diversity conservation", but SBSTTA 3 did not explicitly incorporate this element into its recommendations. Rather, SBSTTA 3 incorporated into the work programme the additional considerations identified by COP 3, i.e. on methodologies for criteria and indicators and on analysis of human influences (see above).

Moreover, by suggesting that the "remaining research and technological priorities identified in the SBSTTA Recommendation II" be taken into consideration as future work is developed, SBSTTA 3 appears to have further weakened and delayed action. In many ways the approach taken by the Parties at SBSTTA 3 reflect the discussions on the appropriate forum to address forest-related issues, and the concern expressed by some Parties to avoid duplication and overlap with work being undertaken by the IFF (see further section 4.3 below).

As noted above, COP 4 adopted the work programme largely based on the recommendations of SBSTTA. While the development of the work programme indicates a progressive weakening and deferral of action, the adoption of the work programme in itself marks an important step forward in addressing forest-related issues under the Convention. A number of positive elements are included, presenting opportunities to further progress work on forest biological diversity. In particular, the COP specifically called on the GEF to give a "high priority" to work relating to forests.

3. Guidance to the Global Environment Facility

As mentioned above, the GEF is the institutional structure operating the financial mechanism of the Convention on an interim basis. Funding through the GEF is to be provided on the basis of policy, strategy, eligibility criteria and programme priorities. Guidance on these issues is provided to the GEF by the COP.

The GEF has established an Operational Programme on forest ecosystems.[48] To date the GEF has relied on guidance by the COP mainly in relation to the implementation of Article 6 (national plans, strategies and programmes) and Article 8 (*in situ* conservation) of the Convention as the basis for its programme on forest ecosystems. In a first set of guidance provided to it by COP 1,[49] the GEF identified the following of relevance to forests:

- projects that promote the conservation and sustainable use of biological diversity ... in other environmentally vulnerable areas...; and

---

[48] The objective of the Operational Programme on forest ecosystems (GEF Operational Programme Number 3) is the conservation and sustainable use of the biological resources in forest ecosystems. Conservation or *in situ* protection is to be sought through protection of primary/old growth and ecologically mature secondary forest ecosystems, by establishing and strengthening systems of conservation areas, focusing primarily on tropical and temperate ecosystems in areas at risk. Sustainable use forest management is to be sought by combining production, socio-economic, and biological diversity goals. GEF resources are used to meet the incremental costs of activities in this Operational Programme.

[49] UNEP/CBD/COP/I/17, Policy, Strategy, Programme Priorities and Eligibility Criteria for access to and utilization of financial resources of the Convention on Biological Diversity, Annex 1.

- projects that promote the conservation and/or sustainable use of endemic species.

COP 2 approved a second set of guidance, concerning, *inter alia*, finance for measures for conservation and sustainable use and for *in situ* conservation, and preliminary consideration of components of biological diversity particularly under threat. As noted above, COP 2 also considered a number of general issues related to forests and biological diversity.[50]

More significantly, COP 4 decided that the GEF should "provide adequate and timely financial support to Parties for projects and capacity-building activities for implementing the programme of work of forest biological diversity at the national, regional and subregional levels and the use of the clearing-house mechanism to include activities that contribute to halting and addressing deforestation, basic assessments and monitoring of forest biological diversity, including taxonomic studies and inventories, focusing on forest species, other important components of forest biological diversity and ecosystems under threat".[51]

Moreover, as mentioned above, COP 4 urged Parties, the GEF and other financial institutions to give "high priority" to the allocation of resources to activities that advance the objectives of the Convention in relation to forest biological diversity.[52]

The current portfolio of GEF projects lists some 45 projects under the forest ecosystem programme, although this does not include biodiversity projects, under other programmes, which are relevant to forests.

The GEF Corporate Business Plan[53] notes that significant efforts are underway to protect and sustainably manage forest ecosystems, and that these will be increased in accordance with guidance from COP 4. Resource allocation for the Operational Programme on Forest Ecosystems has amounted to US $312 million, including the Pilot Phase, making this the largest Operational Programme within the biodiversity focal area.[54] The GEF Corporate Business Plan further notes that most of the focus of the forest ecosystem programme to date "has been in tropical humid forests, with some projects including parts of dry tropical and temperate broad leave forests and very few in coniferous forests". It provides that there is scope to include a larger representation of forest types, particularly in developing countries, and that greater attention is needed to projects on alien species, agro-biodiversity in forests, planning and implementation of projects by indigenous people, and assessment of natural disturbances. The GEF is currently analysing the guidance from COP 4 in relation to the forests work programme.

4. Other CBD Activities Relevant to Forests

In addition to work being undertaken within the context of the thematic work programme on forests, a number of other activities under the Convention are potentially of relevance to forest biological diversity and should be noted. In particular, work undertaken in relation to specific issues such as the implementation of Article 8(j) and related provisions of the Convention on indigenous and local communities, the implementation of the provisions on access to genetic resources and benefit-sharing, as well as cross-cutting issues such as work related to the ecosystem approach, on alien species, on indicators and on incentive measures are all of potential relevance to forest conservation

---

[50] Decision II/9, Annex.

[51] Decision VI/13.

[52] Decision IV/7.

[53] GEF Corporate Business Plan FY00-FY02, GEF/C.12/11, September 11, 1998.

[54] *Id.* at 9. As of June 1998, the actual allocation was $309.938 million.

and sustainable management. In addition, the application of the Convention's thematic work programme on marine and coastal biological diversity to mangroves is of relevance.[55]

As mentioned above, the Convention recognises the importance of indigenous and local communities to the conservation and sustainable use of biological diversity in several of its provisions. These call on the Parties to the CBD to respect, preserve and maintain knowledge, innovations and practices of indigenous and local communities and to protect and encourage customary use of biological resources.[56] Emphasis is also placed on the right of indigenous and local communities to share in the benefits derived from the use of their resources, knowledge and innovations. COP 3 stressed the need to implement Article 8(j) and related provisions, and initiated an inter-sessional process to further develop these provisions.[57] COP 4 built on this initiative by establishing an *ad hoc* open-ended inter-sessional working group to, *inter alia*, advise on the application and development of legal and other appropriate forms of protection for the knowledge, innovations and practices of indigenous and local communities embodying traditional lifestyles relevant for the conservation and sustainable use of biological diversity. The working group is to report directly to the COP and to advise, where appropriate, SBSTTA.[58]

COP 4 also established a panel of experts on access to genetic resources and benefit-sharing, which has the mandate to develop a common understanding of basic concepts and to explore all options for addressing the issue of access and benefit-sharing on mutually agreed terms, including by the development of guiding principles, guidelines and codes of best practice. The work of the panel will include considerations of issues relevant to forest genetic resources. GEF resources will be made available for additional work on access to genetic resources and benefit-sharing.[59]

In relation to cross-cutting issues, COP 4 confirmed that the ecosystem approach should be the framework within which to carry out the analysis and implementation of the objectives of the Convention, and the elaboration and implementation of the various thematic areas and cross-cutting work under the Convention.[60] COP 4 further acknowledged that, despite repeated references to the ecosystem approach, there was still a need to develop a workable definition and to further elaborate the ecosystem approach. It requested the SBSTTA to develop principles and other guidance on the approach and report on its progress to COP 5.[61]

Similarly, COP 4 noted that the problems associated with the introduction of alien species is another cross-cutting issue which needed to be addressed as an integrated component of the various

---

[55] Decision IV/5 adopted a programme of work with the aim of promoting implementation of the Jakarta Mandate on Marine and Coastal Biological Diversity (adopted at COP 2). The programme identifies important operational objectives and priority activities within the framework of five key programme elements: integrated marine and coastal area management; marine and coastal living resources; marine and coastal protected areas; mariculture; and alien species. The programme provides a framework for activities to implement the Jakarta Mandate until the year 2000.

[56] Article 8(j), 10(c).

[57] As part of this process, a meeting was held prior to COP 4 from 24 to 28 November 1997, in Madrid: Workshop on Traditional Knowledge and Biological Diversity.

[58] Decision IV/9.

[59] Decision IV/8.

[60] Decision IV/1

[61] A workshop on the ecosystem approach was held in Lilongwe, Malawi, from 26 to 28 January 1998 (UNEP/CBD/4/Inf.9). SBSTTA was requested to take into account the conclusions and recommendations of the workshop.

sectoral and thematic items under the COP's programme of work. It requested SBSTTA to develop guiding principles for the prevention, introduction and mitigation of the impacts of alien species for the next COP. Parties have been invited to develop country-driven projects and to incorporate activities to address alien species into their national strategies, programmes and action plans. COP 4 also requested the GEF to provide adequate and timely support for such projects.[62]

Work being currently undertaken in respect of biological diversity assessments and indicator development (relevant to the implementation of Article 7 on the identification of the components of biological diversity), and on incentive measures will also be of particular relevance to forest conservation and sustainable management. On indicators, in addition to the work identified within the context of the programme of work on forest biological diversity (see above), work on a core set of indicators of biological diversity, particularly those related to threats is currently ongoing.[63] COP 4 endorsed the recommendation of SBSTTA 3 on work relating to indicators.[64] As part of its first phase the work programme calls for the development of a menu of indicators in the thematic areas, including forests.[65]

Similarly, with regards to work on incentive measures COP 4, *inter alia*, encouraged Parties as a first step towards formulating such measures to identify threats to biological diversity and underlying causes of biological diversity loss, and to develop legal and policy frameworks for the design and implementation of incentive measures.[66]

IV. Issues and Challenges Affecting Consideration of Forest Biological Diversity under the CBD

The previous sections have summarised the potential application of the CBD to forests and have outlined some of the relevant action taken under the Convention to date on forest biological diversity. This section attempts to identify some of the factors which have affected the consideration of forest biological diversity under the CBD. This involves examination of both general and specific issues, which can broadly be divided into the following categories: (i) the nature of the Convention; (ii) institutional issues relating to the Convention, including the approach to further work adopted by the Conference of the Parties; and (iii) specific challenges arising in relation to the consideration of forests.

1. The Nature of the Convention

The text of the Convention offers both opportunities and challenges for action to conserve and sustainable use forest biological diversity. On the one hand, the provisions contained in the Convention are legally binding, and the comprehensive language of the Convention clearly

---

[62] Decision IV/1.

[63] SBSTTA Recommendation II/1, as endorsed by COP 3 (Decision III/10) recommended work to be undertaken on a core set of indicators of biological diversity, particularly those under threat. A liaison group meeting was subsequently held on indicators in June 1997. SBSTTA 3 elaborated a work programme on indicators based on a two-track approach, see UNEP/CBD/COP/4/2 p.53.

[64] Decision IV/1.

[65] Recommendation III/5.

[66] Decision IV/10.

includes within its scope all types of forest biological diversity, although it is not limited to forests. The Convention adopts a holistic ecosystem approach to the conservation and sustainable use of biological diversity. This is evidenced for example in the requirement to integrate biological diversity into sectoral and cross-sectoral plans and programmes, and into decision-making.[67] It makes reference to certain fundamental principles, which would appear to support action to conserve and sustainable use forests, such as the affirmation that the conservation of biological diversity is a "common concern of mankind", and the recognition that a precautionary approach is needed where there is a threat of significant reduction or loss of biological diversity. Crucially, as noted above, the Convention provides a financial mechanism for the provision of new and additional financial resources to developing countries Parties to meet the agreed incremental costs of implementing the Convention. Although not strictly speaking a "framework" Convention, the CBD was conceived as a framework for future elaboration of more specific obligations.[68]

On the other hand, as is well known, the obligations contained in the Convention are heavily qualified. Thus although the Convention's provisions are clearly applicable to forest biological diversity, in most cases those provisions do not impose hard specific obligations on Parties. The provisions are to a large extent soft, and rely on further elaboration at the national level through national strategies and action plans, and at the international level through further elaboration by the COP.

Moreover, although the Convention adopts a much-heralded holistic or comprehensive approach to the conservation and sustainable use of biological diversity, including that contained in forests, this holistic approach may in itself have posed problems for the formulation of specific action. Translating the holistic approach into concrete action in the light of incomplete scientific knowledge has proved difficult. This may in part explain the pace of progress under the Convention, and the tendency to focus initially upon scientific input and assessments and upon increasing understanding of the ecosystem approach within the thematic areas.

The reference to common concern in the preamble of the Convention is counter-balanced by the emphasis upon sovereignty over natural resources, including of course forests within national jurisdiction, both in the preamble and in the operative part of the Convention.

As noted above, the Convention establishes a framework for future action by the Parties at the national and international level. At the international level, this requires, among other things, elaboration of the Conventions provisions through the institutional arrangements established under the Convention. However, the country-driven approach inherent in the Convention has tended to make priority-setting at the level of the Convention's institutions difficult. Priority-setting exercises have tended to result in "shopping lists" rather than meaningful prioritisation. Coupled with the enormous scope of the Convention's agenda, as a result of its comprehensive mandate, the failure to prioritise has also served to hamper meaningful action in particular areas. It is of course fair to comment that had there existed a real political will to take action on a particular issue, these challenges might have been effectively overcome. In the case of forests, however, there has been scope for those Parties wishing to avoid action under the CBD to delay any such action.

---

[67] Articles 6(b) and 10(a).

[68] *See* further Françoise Burhenne-Guilmin and Susan Casey-Lefkowitz, "The Convention on Biological Diversity: A Hard Won Global Achievement", 3 Yearbook of International Environmental Law, (1992) p.43; Lyle Glowka, Françoise Burhenne-Guilmin and Hugh Synge, A Guide to the Convention on Biological Diversity, (IUCN Environmental Law Centre, 1994).

2. Institutional and Process Relevant Issues

This section focuses initially on general aspects of the approach adopted by the Conference of the Parties to the elaboration and review of the Convention. It considers on a preliminary basis a number of factors:

- the medium-term programme of work;

- the thematic approach and the development of work programmes;

- mandates and functioning of CBD institutions;

- the role of the CBD.

2.1 The Medium-Term Programme of Work

As noted above, at its first meeting the COP adopted its medium-term programme of work for 1994-1997, with a view to adopting a longer-term programme of work and reviewing the operations of the Convention in 1997.[69] It is striking that forest biological diversity did not feature in terms on the medium-term programme of work, and was not due to be considered until 1996 under the agenda item, terrestrial biological diversity. Even in 1996, the ecosystem focus of the COP (see below) was due to be agricultural biological diversity, with the consideration of terrestrial biological diversity taking place within the context of the consideration of outcomes of deliberations on that issue by the CSD. Indeed it has been noted that forests were "an almost unmentionable topic" at COP 1.[70] As outlined in section 3.2 above, initial work on forests was undertaken under the agenda item "components of biological diversity particularly under threat".

2.2 The Thematic Approach and Development of Work Programmes

Under its medium-term programme of work, the COP adopted a thematic approach, with certain standing items to be considered at each COP, and thematic areas, i.e. particular ecosystems to feature on the agenda on a rotating basis. The first ecosystem focus was marine and coastal biological diversity, and the treatment of this issue at COP 2 and subsequently has influenced the approach of the COP to the other ecosystems considered, including forests. In particular, there has been a clear tendency to focus initially on the elaboration of a work programme on each ecosystem for the Convention, and thus work programmes now exist in relation to marine and coastal biological diversity,[71] agricultural biological diversity,[72] inland water biological diversity,[73] and of course forest biological diversity.[74] While there is apparent consistency in this approach, the rationale for the existence of a work programme and the content of the particular work programmes, is not always clear. In particular, the products or outcomes of the work programmes are not always identified. It is also not entirely clear in what ways the thematic work programmes are to interact

---

[69] Decision I/9.

[70] *See* Earth Negotiations Bulletin's summary of COP 2, at p.9.

[71] Decision IV/5.

[72] Decision III/11.

[73] Decision IV/4.

[74] Decision IV/7.

with processes and ongoing work addressing cross-cutting issues, such as the working group on traditional knowledge,[75] the expert panel on access to genetic resources,[76] and work on indicators.[77] As noted in section 3.4 above, each of these cross-cutting issues are likely to involve significant consideration of forest biological diversity.

2.3   Institutional Issues

Part of the review of operation of the Convention also involves considering the institutional mandates of the Convention's organs. Particular concerns have been expressed about the functioning of the Convention's scientific and technical advisory body, SBSTTA. These concerns have essentially related to the political nature of the SBSTTA to date.[78] SBSTTA has yet to find satisfactory and effective working arrangements, although a revised modus operandi for SBSTTA was adopted at COP 4.[79] Its agenda has tended to mirror that of the COP. Given its workload, it has been difficult to find adequate time within the one-week SBSTTA meeting to address all issues in detail. There has been a need for some intersessional work, through mechanisms foreseen in the modus operandi of SBSTTA (which was initially endorsed by the COP in Decision II/1), such as expert panels and liaison groups. However, in the absence of clear guidance as to how intersessional groups should be constituted, concerns have been expressed about transparency of these intersessional activities. Although, following the approach taken by COP 2 in its decision on marine and coastal biological diversity,[80] the Secretariat has attempted to establish rosters of experts in the various thematic areas, including forests, by inviting Parties to submit the names of experts for the roster, the Secretariat has not received guidance as to how to use the roster. Certain Parties have therefore questioned the selection procedures for the liaison groups, particularly the forest group which met in May 1997. These concerns have tended to delay progress – for example, at SBSTTA 3 a number of Parties expressed concerns about the lack of transparency in relation to the liaison group meeting on forest biological diversity, and ultimately reopened the proposed work programme which had been developed following the guidance of the liaison group.

2.4   Role of the CBD

The lack of clarity in the purpose and products of the work programmes reflects a deeper lack of certainty about the role of the Convention itself. In the context of the review of operations of the Convention for COP 4, concerns began to be raised about the lack of strategic focus of the Convention. No common view appears to have emerged among the Parties and stakeholders on what it is that the Convention should be producing, and who these products should be aimed at. In its early phase, the responses of the COP and SBSTTA has largely been to focus on an initial scoping of issues, and on seeking to develop institutions to meet the needs of the Convention.

---

[75]   Decision IV/9.

[76]   Decision IV/8.

[77]   Decision IV/1 and SBSTTA Recommendation III/5.

[78]   *See* Report on the informal Meeting on Issues Dealing with the Operation of SBSTTA; UNEP/CBD/COP/4/2, Annex 3, where the scientific, technical and technological role of SBSTTA was emphasised. It was generally considered that SBSTTA has to date been less successful in providing the detailed information needed to support decision-making or national efforts to implement the Convention.

[79]   Decision IV/16, paragraph 11.

[80]   Decision II/10.

Instead of focusing on strategic issues relating to moving from scoping to concrete action and outputs, discussion at COP 4 on the review of operations of the Convention tended to focus largely on structural questions, such as whether new standing bodies should be established. The intersessional meeting on the review of operations of the Convention scheduled for June 1999,[81] and the forthcoming re-consideration of this issue at COP 5 are likely to constitute important steps in determining the future nature and outputs of the Convention.

3. The Impact of the IPF on the CBD

In relation specifically to the treatment of forest biological diversity under the Convention, the establishment of the IPF and its successor, the IFF, has been a key factor. As has been noted, the medium-term programme of work adopted by the COP at its first meeting did not envisage any consideration of forest biological diversity until COP 3, under the item terrestrial biological diversity. However, the establishment of the IPF by the CSD in 1995 prompted calls for earlier action under the CBD, specifically in the form of input into the IPF on forest biological diversity.

The initial input of the CBD COP into the IPF process has been outlined in section 3.1 above. In addition to its input in relation to traditional forest-related knowledge, the focus from the perspective of the CBD was largely on calling for the IPF to take into account forest biological diversity considerations in its work. However, while the existence of the IPF may have initially prompted a consideration of forests under the CBD, it has also served to create a diversion from concrete progress under the Convention. Much of the discussion on forest in the CBD has been devoted to debating the respective mandates and competence of the CBD and IPF, with a number of Parties arguing that the CBD should await the outcomes of the IPF prior to taking action on forest biological diversity. As illustrated in section 3.2, these debates were particularly evident at SBSTTA 3 (despite its scientific mandate), in discussions on the proposed work programme on forests. Some Parties proposed that the CBD work programme should be "in line with" the IPF, ITFF and future discussions in the IFF. Others took the position that the CBD should not be limited by decisions which had yet to be taken in other fora. Eventually, the Parties agreed that the work programme activities should be "consistent with the proposals for action of the IPF and in close cooperation with the IFF and other related fora".[82] The IFF interim Secretariat itself suggested at SBSTTA 3 that it was premature for the SBSTTA and COP to adopt a work programme on forests before the IFF had made a contribution.[83] By contrast it has been suggested that the COP should be proactive vis-à-vis the IPF/IFF, rather than simply reacting to the IFF agenda, in particular in relation to action that relates more specifically to the conservation aspects of forest biological diversity.

Thus the existence of the IPF has provided scope for delay under the CBD, without itself delivering action for the conservation and sustainable use of forest biological diversity. Interestingly, although the CBD has now adopted a work programme on forests, as noted at the end of section 3.3 the content and timing of that work programme itself appears implicitly at least to await the conclusions of the CSD based on IFF recommendations. The content of the forest work programme itself appears to envisage further inputs from CBD to IFF. It must be asked whether it is appropriate that the role of the CBD be limited to making scientific inputs into another process.

In addition to IPF/IFF considerations, the political obstacles to action on forest biological diversity under the CBD appear to largely reflect the barriers experienced in other fora. In the case of the CBD, as noted earlier, these objections can be backed up by reference to certain basic

---

[81] Decision IV/16.

[82] Recommendation III/3.

[83] *See* Earth Negotiations Bulletin, Vol. 9, No. 73, p.9.

principles under the Convention and its emphasis on national priorities. At COP 4, in discussions on the longer-term programme of work of the Convention, and specifically on the agendas of the next three COP meetings, certain Parties refused to countenance addressing forests again at COP 5, albeit that forests ecosystems have not yet formally been the focus of a COP meeting.

V. Prospects for Future Action on Forest Biological Diversity under the CBD

In the near term the prospects for action on forest biological diversity under the CBD depend upon the implementation and outcomes of the forest work programme. Although the adoption of any work programme on forest might be seen as an achievement many have expressed disappointment at the content of the work programme, particularly in the light of what was initially recommended by the liaison group. There is some scope for positive action under the work programme however, especially for example in relation to criteria and indicators for forest biological diversity.

It might be noted, however, that the forest work programme, in contrast to the other thematic work programmes, does not envisage a central role for the Secretariat in carrying out the activities. Instead the Parties are exhorted to support relevant activities, and thus the outcome of the work programme in the initial phases at least is likely to depend on the willingness of Parties to support it. This may be of concern given the competing demands of the IFF for inputs and activities. One particular positive aspect however, which might contribute to enhancing further action on forest biological diversity, is the potential availability of financial resources from the Global Environment Facility in line with its Operational Programme on forest ecosystems (see section 3.3 above). However, the apparent lack of a 'driving force' for the forests work programme must be of some concern. Although the Secretariat will probably, in accordance with any guidance from the COP and SBSTTA Bureaux, undertake work to support the work programme, the attention which can be focused on the work programme may be limited by the fact that the focus of COP 5 will be other terrestrial ecosystems, drylands, grasslands, savannah and arid ecosystems.[84]

As mentioned above, the Parties at COP 4 did not agree to the establishment of an *ad hoc* technical expert group on forests, leaving any such decision for SBSTTA to take. As part of the review of operations of the Convention, SBSTTA is to provide COP 5 with advice on the terms of reference for *ad hoc* technical expert groups on thematic areas, taking into account the programme of work adopted for COPs 5 to 7.[85] There is scope therefore for an expert panel on forest biological diversity under SBSTTA to contribute to the implementation of the work programme on forest biological diversity, and for its advice on status and trends of forest biological diversity to be submitted to COP 6.

However, as noted above, certain timing issues arise, in that forest biological diversity is not now due to be the thematic focus of the COP until its sixth meeting, which is not likely to be until 2002, or at the earliest 2001. This is of course after the CSD is due to consider the IFF's recommendations, which, regardless of any the legal debates as to the relationship between the two institutions, is likely in reality to be pivotal in determining the content of the second phase of the CBD forest work programme.

To date it has been difficult to assess what action, if any, is being taken at the national level on forest biological diversity. One reason for this is that the guidelines for the first national reports of Parties only require general information on the implementation of Article 6 of the Convention.

---

[84] Decision IV.16.

[85] Decision IV/16, paragraphs 21 and 16.

In the context of current discussions on the format and content of future national reports, COP 4 has requested SBSTTA to advise the next meeting of the COP on, *inter alia*, the nature of information to be included in the second national reports.[86] In discussion relating to the scope of the second national reports, there has been some suggestions that focus should be on the implementation of Article 7 of the Convention on identification and monitoring. In this context the CBD might usefully play a role in assessing and monitoring action on the conservation and sustainable use of forest biological diversity. It should be noted that under the CBD there is an obligation to provide national reports, while the CSD has no specific mandate to require reporting.

Lastly, work under the Convention on cross-cutting issues such as, on indicators, access and benefit-sharing and traditional knowledge present particular prospects for making progress on the conservation and sustainable use of forest biological diversity.

VI. Conclusions

The existence of the IPF and its successor, the IFF has no doubt been a key factor in the consideration of forest-related issues under the CBD. While the IPF/IFF process has served, on the one hand, to catalyse action under the CBD on forest biological diversity, it has also served, on the other hand, to divert attention away from the Convention in matters relating to forests conservation and sustainable use. Although a forests work programme has now been adopted, the emphasis is on synergy, cooperation with, and avoiding the duplication of work currently envisaged under the auspices of, the IFF. In many ways, the work programme is framed in language which envisages a role for the Convention as contributing to the implementation of the IPF proposals for action, particularly where these call for input from the CBD.

In the near term, action under the CBD on forest biological diversity will primarily depend on the implementation of the forest work programme. Despite its limitations, the programme of work marks a first step in a longer-term strategy to implement the objectives of the Convention as they relate to forests biological diversity. As a rolling work programme it will come under review at every subsequent COP and will be the particular focus of the sixth meeting of the COP. Accordingly, the potential to strengthen action on forest biological diversity exists, including the possibility of establishing an expert group on forests under SBSTTA. While the Parties at COP 4 were unable to agree on the establishment of such an expert group, there was nevertheless support for its establishment. At its next meeting SBSTTA is likely therefore to consider the matter again. Moreover, the potential for accessing GEF resources is also a significant element.

Furthermore, work under the Convention on other cross-cutting issues, in particular on the provisions of the Convention relating to indigenous and local communities, on criteria and indicators, on incentive measures and on access to genetic resources and benefit-sharing also present particular opportunities to advance work relating to forest conservation and sustainable management.

However, the fact that COP 6 is not likely to be held after the CSD has considered the recommendations of the IFF in the year 2000, and the fact that the forests work programme is structured in such a way that the initial focus is on research, suggests that the potential for more concrete action on forests might need to await the deliberations and outcomes of the IFF process. These factors ultimately question the degree to which there can be any immediate and effective implementation of the forests work programme under the Convention.

---

[86] Decision IV/14.

Global Forest Policy and
Selected International Instruments:
A Preliminary Review

By David R. Downes *

---

*   Chris Wold prepared the discussion of CITES and Richard Tarasofsky prepared the one on the Desertification Convention. Initial drafts of other sections were prepared by Kristen Genovese (climate change) and Braden Penhoet (Ramsar Convention). Helpful suggestions and comments on drafts were received from Natalie Eddy, Don Goldberg, Korinna Horta, David Hunter, Bill Mankin, Simon Rietbergen, Carole St. Laurent, Bella Sewall, Richard Tarasofsky, and Chris Wold. Tiffany Donovan deserves special thanks for extensive editorial assistance. Information was provided by many individuals associated with or knowledgeable about the institutions, instruments and initiatives discussed in this paper.

I.   Introduction

This paper outlines some of the major global instruments relevant to forests in relation to several general categories: conservation, indigenous peoples, international trade and investment, and climate change.[1] It should be noted that none of the legal instruments was specifically designed to address forests. Nevertheless, forests are related to their goals and programmes. In addition, it was considered appropriate to discuss two non-legal initiatives within the context of these categories: the Forest Stewardship Council and the International Organization for Standardization.

By reviewing the status of implementation of each entity's forest-related mandate, this report seeks to build upon IUCN's earlier analytical work in this area.[2] This chapter does not purport to be an exhaustive review, but highlights activities of significant players in order to give readers a sense of the richness of activity already underway in other forums, in particular to help the decision-makers at the IFF draw on this experience in defining the IFF's recommendations.

For each instrument this chapter seeks to identify the following elements:

- The mandate of each institution and its relationship to the conservation and sustainable management of forests;

- The forest and forestry-related programmes and the human and financial resources for these programmes;

- The strength and weakness of each institution with respect to matters such as the technical competence of staff, financial resources, and political support for its mandate;

- The potential for future success and the identification of obstacles that might block progress on implementation of forest-related programmes or obligations.

However, resources were not available to complete the assessment of each of these elements for each instrument. Thus, in many instances, the paper identifies the need for further research and analysis and suggests possible avenues for future research.

II.   Conservation of Forests

This section reviews instruments and programmes most prominently relating to conservation of forests. It should be noted that there are no instruments to date that address sustainable forest management.

Forests are complex communities of many different species of organisms coexisting in and on a given area of land. Thus, the conservation instruments most relevant to forests involve the protection of designated areas of the earth's surface. It is generally recognized that "protected areas" form an important part of many strategies for conserving the ecological integrity and biological diversity of the world's forests.

---

[1]   These categories comprise most of the international tools devised to date to work on the main problems confronting forests. However, we recognize that this classification does not necessarily capture every relevant tool. In particular, the limited resources available for this study did not allow us to cover the activity of crisis management or emergency response.

[2]   *See* particularly Richard Tarasofsky, *The International Forests Regime: Legal and policy issues* (Gland, Switzerland: IUCN, 1995).

In protected areas, uses of the forest and activities within it are in principle strictly limited. Generally, regulations in protected areas do not permit commercial harvesting of timber or other forest products. Of the world's remaining forests, it is estimated that 13.3% of mangrove forests, 11.7% of tropical forests, and 6.0% of nontropical forests are included in protected areas.[3] Data on the effectiveness of enforcement of protective measures are difficult to obtain. It appears, however, that many protected forest areas are to a greater or lesser degree "paper parks," and that illegal logging, mining, and forest clearing are widespread.

Further research would be useful on the extent to which the extent of protected areas shelters a sufficient selection of ecosystem types and an area adequate to protect valuable ecosystem functions and processes, such as regeneration of biological resources and maintenance of ecosystem services.

Activities at the international level have been successful in promoting the concept of protected areas. International conferences and networks have been useful in communicating a wealth of information and experience. International institutions have contributed by promoting guidelines on best practices and standards, developing standard indexes and criteria for classifying and evaluating protected areas, providing valuable technical assistance, and defining and managing transboundary protected areas. Perhaps the most widely used and recognized international system for categorizing protected areas is that developed and maintained by IUCN.[4] Limited financial assistance has also been made available through international instruments. It is not entirely clear whether and how these instruments have contributed significantly to enforcement and compliance on the ground or whether their main contribution so far has been in the development of principles and standards.

Several international instruments and programmes exist which are relevant to the protected areas approach to forest conservation. They include the Ramsar Convention, the World Heritage Convention, and the Man and the Biosphere (MAB) Programme of the United Nations Educational, Scientific and Cultural Organization (UNESCO). Although these instruments are important for the implementation of the protected areas approach, they only reach small subsets of the total forest areas in need of protection. The Convention on Biological Diversity (CBD), in contrast, has the potential to support the development of a more comprehensive approach to protected areas for forests and other ecosystems, but its work, especially its work on forest biodiversity, is still in the early stages of development. For further discussion of the CBD and forests, see the companion chapter on that topic in this volume.

1. Ramsar Convention on Wetlands

Mangrove forests – among the most threatened of the world's forest types – are situated in coastal wetlands. The Ramsar Convention on Wetlands of International Importance especially as Waterfowl Habitat (the Ramsar Convention) aims to promote the protection and "wise use" of

---

[3]   *See* World Resources Institute, *World Resources 1998-99* (New York: Oxford University Press, 1998), at 295. Protected areas include areas protected as defined under IUCN categories I-V.

[4]   *See* IUCN, *Guidelines for Protected Area Management Categories* (Gland: IUCN, 1994). A summary of the IUCN categories is available from the World Conservation Monitoring Centre's web site at <http://www.wcmc.org.uk/protected_areas/data/sample/iucn_cat.htm> Also widely used are the guidelines for the UNESCO Man and the Biosphere Programme, within the growing network of UNESCO biosphere reserves.

wetland areas[5] within the territorial boundaries of party nation-states. In order to become a Party to the Convention, a nation must designate at least one wetland site for management as a nature preserve, subject to a standard of "wise use" defined in terms of "sustainable utilization."[6] Article 3.2 of the Convention calls on parties to monitor changes in the "ecological character" of wetlands within their territories. The 1993 COP called for development of standardized definitions and guidelines for characterizing and monitoring changes in wetland ecology.[7]

Initially, the Convention focused on wetlands which had international significance because they were habitat for migratory waterfowl. Over time, however, the Convention's mandate has evolved in an effort to embrace the broader implications of wetland destruction.

As a result, increasing attention has been given to forested wetlands, in particular the rapidly disappearing tropical mangrove forests around the world. Mangrove forests, found along tropical coastlines, are highly productive and serve as important resources for many local communities.[8] They are, however, seriously at risk. It has been estimated that 50% of the world's mangrove forests have been destroyed or seriously degraded over the past decade.[9] The 1996-99 work plan produced by Ramsar's Scientific and Technical Review Panel provides for consultations on whether to develop criteria for monitoring status and changes in ecological conditions in specific types of wetlands, including mangroves.[10]

At Brisbane in 1996, the COP adopted a Strategic Plan for 1997-2002, incorporating ambitious non-binding goals for advancing awareness about wetlands and improving planning, monitoring and management of listed and non-listed wetland sites. One of the goals outlined in the Strategic Plan is to "give priority attention to the designation of new sites from wetland types currently underrepresented on the Ramsar List, and in particular, when appropriate, coral reefs, *mangroves,*

---

[5] The Ramsar Convention defines wetlands as "areas of marsh, fen, peatland or water, whether natural or artificial, permanent or temporary, with water that is static or flowing, fresh, brackish or salt, including areas of marine water the depth of which at low tide does not exceed six meters" (Article 1.1). The Convention further provides that areas of concern for purposes of the Convention "incorporate riparian and coastal zones adjacent to the wetlands, and islands or bodies of marine water deeper than six meters at low tide lying within the wetlands" (Article 2.1) . Though precise data are difficult to obtain, estimates suggest that roughly 6 percent of the world's land area can be classified as wetlands, or about 5.7 million square kilometers. Ramsar Information Paper no.1, published by the Ramsar Convention Bureau, Gland, Switzerland.

[6] Wise use is mentioned in Article 2. Defining language was adopted by the Conference of the Parties of the Ramsar Convention, Regina, Canada, 1987 (quoted in Ramsar Information Paper no.7, published by the Ramsar Convention Bureau, Gland, Switzerland).

[7] Tim Jones, "Convention On Wetlands – 25 Years; Ecological Character – Introduction," in The Ramsar Newsletter, Issue 22, January, 1996. A report by the Scientific and Technical Review Panel (STRP) was accepted by the Brisbane COP as providing "working definitions, to be assessed further during the 1997-1999 triennium, of 'ecological character' and 'change in ecological character.'" Resolution VI.1 of the 6th Meeting of the Conference of the Contracting Parties, Brisbane, Australia, 19-27 March 1996.

[8] A. Charlotte de Fontaubert, David R. Downes, and Tundi Agardy, *Biodiversity in the Seas: Implementing the Convention on Biological Diversity in Marine and Coastal Habitats* (IUCN 1996), at 27, *republished in* 10 GEORGETOWN INTERNATIONAL ENVIRONMENTAL LAW REVIEW 753 (1998).

[9] *See id.* (citation omitted).

[10] 14 STRP Work Plan 1996-1999, para 10.a.

seagrass beds and peatlands."[11] Reflecting an increased awareness of the values and needs of indigenous peoples dependent on forest ecologies, the Ramsar Strategic Plan also aims to involve local communities in the management of wetlands, incorporating "traditional knowledge and management practice of indigenous people and local communities in the conservation and wise use of wetlands."[12]

To date, a total of 931 wetland sites, comprising a total of 69 million hectares of land, are included in the Ramsar List of Wetlands of International Importance. Mangrove forests are present in approximately one-third of these sites, including approximately 596,000 hectares in Bangladesh's Sundarbans, over 54,000 hectares in the Caicos Islands, over 35,000 hectares in Ecuador, and some 12,000 hectares in Suriname.[13] Further research is needed on the extent to which these sites are effectively protected.

In addition, the IFF Secretariat makes the suggestion that the Ramsar Convention could be an appropriate instrument to give effect to the recommendation of the XI World Forestry Congress (October 1997) that governments pay more attention to mangrove and coastal forest systems.[14]

Ramsar entered into force in 1975. It had 112 Contracting Parties as of 4 August 1998. The Convention is administered by a secretariat called the Ramsar Bureau, under the direction of the Conference of the Contracting Parties (COP), which is advised by a Scientific and Technical Review Panel (STRP). Parties submit public reports on their implementation of Convention obligations to triennial COPs. Further research is needed on the human and financial resources available for carrying out forest-related programmes of work, and on the strengths and weaknesses of the Convention in terms of forests. This could involve interviews with selected officials of the Ramsar Bureau, officials of active governments, and individuals in organizations familiar with relevant protected areas, which might include groups such as IUCN's World Commission on Protected Areas or the World Conservation Monitoring Centre.

2. World Heritage Convention[15]

The objective of the Convention Concerning the Protection of the World Cultural and Natural Heritage (WHC) is to create international support for the protection and maintenance of sites demonstrating outstanding cultural and natural heritage of universal value. It provides for identification and protection of such sites under international law and encourages public and official attention to the value of its stated objective.

Each Party to the WHC is obligated to identify, protect, conserve and transmit to future generations its unique cultural and natural heritage. Some national courts have interpreted the

---

[11] Convention on Wetlands (Ramsar, Iran, 1971) Strategic Plan 1997-2002, adopted by the 6th Meeting of the Conference of the Contracting Parties (Brisbane, Australia, 19-27 March 1996) [hereinafter Strategic Plan], at para. 6.2.3 (emphasis added).

[12] Strategic Plan, para 2.7.3 and 2.7.4 (via "establishing wetland management committees, especially at Ramsar sites, on which local stakeholders, landowners, managers, developers and community interest groups, in particular women's groups, are represented.")

[13] Peter R. Bacon, *The Role of the Ramsar Convention in Mangrove Management*, INT'L NEWSLETTER OF COASTAL MANAGEMENT (Special Ed. 1, March 1997, pp. 25-26).

[14] IFF Secretariat, *Information on Forest-Related Work Under Existing Instruments*, Background Document 5, July 1998.

[15] Portions of the discussion of the World Heritage Convention are adapted from De Fontaubert, et al., *supra* n. 9, at 63-64.

obligations pursuant to WHC as imposing a legal requirement to protect designated sites under national law. In addition, the World Heritage Commission selects sites nominated by the Parties to be placed on the World Heritage List.

Article 2 of the WHC defines natural heritage to include, *inter alia*, "natural sites or precisely delineated areas of outstanding universal value from the point of view of science, conservation or natural beauty." The Parties revised the criteria for selecting sites in 1994 to provide for identification of sites that are "the most important and significant natural habitats for *in-situ* conservation of biological diversity," or "outstanding examples representing significant on-going ecological and biological processes in the evolution and development of terrestrial ... ecosystems and communities of plants and animals."

As of late 1996 the World Heritage List included 506 sites in a total of 107 countries. This total consisted of 380 cultural sites, 107 natural sites, and 19 mixed natural/cultural sites.[16] Currently over 32 ecologically significant forests are included on the World Heritage List.[17] Further research is needed on the effectiveness of protection of these sites, the relevance of these sites to and their importance to forest protection generally.

The WHC entered into force in 1972. As of April 1998, 153 countries were Parties. The WHC establishes a multilateral World Heritage Fund to finance protection of World Heritage Sites in developing countries party to the Convention, to which developed countries donate about US$ 2-3 million annually. Further research is needed to review the human resources available under the WHC.

The WHC has the capacity to play a significant role in forest protection. In theory, large areas of forest could be designated as sites of universal value. In practice, however, the WHC has been applied to relatively small areas of the earth's surface, with some exceptions such as the Great Barrier Reef of Australia and the barrier reef of Belize. Further research is needed to assess fully the strengths, weaknesses and potential of the WHC with respect to forests. This could involve interviews with selected officials of UNESCO, officials of governments on the World Heritage Committee, and individuals in organizations familiar with relevant protected areas, which might include groups such as those mentioned above in the discussion of Ramsar.

3. The UNESCO Man and the Biosphere Programme (MAB)

The MAB biosphere reserve programme involves a network of "protected areas" voluntarily designated as such by participating governments with the aim of integrating human culture and development with the protection of natural heritage. The network is also intended to facilitate exchange of information among scientists conducting applied research within protected areas. Typically biosphere reserves consist of a restricted core of protected land surrounded by a buffer zone in which economic activity is allowed but is regulated to prevent harm to the core area's biodiversity and ecological integrity.

By 1997 over 337 sites in 85 countries consisting of a total of 200 million hectares have been designated as biosphere reserves.[18] The UNESCO programme has developed standardized criteria pertaining to the management of these reserves. A number of biosphere reserves include forest lands within their boundaries.

---

[16] *See* UNESCO, *World Heritage List*, available on Web site <http://www.unesco.org/whc>

[17] *See supra* n. 15.

[18] *See* Michel Batisse, *Biosphere reserves: a challenge for biodiversity conservation & regional development*, 39(5) ENVIRONMENT (June 1997).

Further research is needed to review the forest-related aspects of the programme, including human and financial resources, and an assessment of their strengths and weaknesses. This could involve interviews with selected officials of UNESCO, officials of governments active in the programme, and individuals in organizations familiar with relevant protected areas issues, which might include groups such as those mentioned above in the discussion of Ramsar.

III. Indigenous Peoples

Many of the world's remaining natural forests are inhabited by indigenous peoples, a term referring generally to people who "were living on their lands before settlers came from elsewhere," or "the descendants ... of those who inhabited a ... region at the time when people of different cultures or ethnic origins arrived, the new arrivals later becoming dominant."[19] It is widely recognized that "many natural forested areas which still survive are today mostly inhabited by indigenous peoples."[20] These peoples frequently depend upon the forest for many aspects of their livelihood and culture. They often employ traditional management systems for land and forests which maintain forest ecosystems and biodiversity at a high level of integrity.

The special relationship between indigenous peoples and forests reflects the special relationship that indigenous peoples have with the land and associated resources. Indigenous peoples consistently emphasize the "spiritual, social, cultural, economic and political significance of lands, territories and resources to the continued survival and vitality of indigenous societies," and the "profound relationship that [they] have to their lands, territories and resources."[21] This intimate relationship has enabled indigenous peoples to build up valuable stores of knowledge and to develop and maintain complex practices and uses that encourage sustainability. Thus, in the words of the Intergovernmental Panel on Forests (IPF), "[t]raditional forest-related knowledge (TFRK) constitutes an important body of knowledge and experience" which "can provide a strong basis for [SFM]."[22]

Deforestation harms the livelihood of indigenous people and the diversity of human culture as well. In the tropics, for example, "deforestation has decimated the indigenous groups that depend on forests for their survival."[23] The IPF noted "with concern" that

---

[19]   United Nations Human Rights Web Site, *Fact Sheet No. 9 (Rev. 1): The Rights of Indigenous Peoples* (Geneva: UN CHR, 1997).

[20]   World Conservation Congress, Montreal, 1996, Resolution 1.55. In the same resolution, IUCN's General Assembly called on IUCN members to support development of forest policy which considers the principle of recognition of the rights of indigenous peoples, including their rights to use the natural resources on their territories in an equitable and ecologically sustainable way. The resolution also called for recognition of the need for effective participation by indigenous peoples in the planning and execution of all activities on their forest lands. The resolution highlighted the two international instruments discussed in this section, the ILO Convention No. 169, and the draft UN declaration on the rights of indigenous peoples.

[21]   U.N. Commission on Human Rights, Human Rights of Indigenous Peoples: Indigenous people and their relationship to land: preliminary working paper, para. 5 (Geneva: UN CHR, 1997) (Doc. No. E/CN.4/Sub.2/1997/17, available on UN Human Rights Center web site <http://www.unhchr.ch/hchr_un.htm>

[22]   IPF Final Report, paras 32, 34.

[23]   Kenton Miller & Laura Tangley, *Trees of Life: Saving Tropical Forests and Their Biological Wealth* at 16 (Boston: Beacon Press, 1991).

some communities with sustainable lifestyles based on TFRK have been undermined by accelerated loss of forests resulting from the introduction of new technological changes and economic pressures, in the absence of adequate measures for conservation and sustainable management. [The IPF] agreed that indigenous people and other forest dependent people embodying traditional lifestyles should play a key role in developing participatory approaches to forest and land management.[24]

1. International Labour Organization (ILO) Convention Nos. 107 and 169

ILO Conventions Nos. 107 and 169 are the only international legal instruments relating exclusively to tribal and indigenous peoples. Convention No. 169 on Indigenous and Tribal Peoples was adopted in 1989 and has been ratified by thirteen countries.[25] Convention No. 107 on Indigenous and Other Tribal and Semi-Tribal Populations was adopted in 1957; it has been superseded by No. 169, but remains in force for twenty countries. These conventions were developed in the ILO framework because there was a perceived need for an international legal instrument regarding indigenous people, and the ILO provided an efficient mechanism for negotiating an agreement.

Convention No. 169 includes several provisions relevant to forests. Perhaps most important are articles 7, 14, and 15.[26] Article 7 provides that indigenous and tribal peoples "shall have the right to decide their own priorities for the process of development," and "shall participate in the formulation, implementation and evaluation of plans and programmes for national and regional development which may affect them directly." It also provides that "[g]overnments shall take measures, in co-operation with the peoples concerned, to protect and preserve the environment of the territories they inhabit."

Article 14, addressing land rights, states that "[t]he rights of ownership and possession of the peoples concerned over the lands which they traditionally occupy shall be recognized." Further, "[g]overnments shall take steps as necessary to identify the lands which the peoples concerned traditionally occupy, and to guarantee effective protection of their rights of ownership and possession."

Finally, Article 15 provides that "[t]he rights of the peoples concerned to the natural resources pertaining to their lands shall be specially safeguarded. These rights include the right of those peoples to participate in the use, management and conservation of these resources." In addition, where the state retains ownership of resources relating to lands, such as sub-surface resources, the

---

[24] The IPF concluded further that "[t]he effective protection of TFRK requires the fair and equitable sharing of benefits among all interested parties including indigenous people and other forest dependent people embodying traditional lifestyles, forest owners and local communities" (para. 35).

[25] These include Bolivia, Colombia, Costa Rica, Denmark, Ecuador, Fiji, Guatemala, Honduras, Mexico, Netherlands, Norway, Paraguay and Peru.

[26] Other relevant provisions include Article 6(1), which provides that governments shall consult in good faith "the peoples concerned, through appropriate procedures and in particular through their representative institutions, whenever consideration is being given to legislative or administrative measures which may affect them directly." Article 16(1) provides that "the peoples concerned shall not be removed from the lands which they occupy," except with their free and informed consent, and subject to other provisions of that article. It has been argued that destruction of a forest on which indigenous people depend constitutes the equivalent of removal and thus is governed by this article.

government shall establish procedures for consulting with indigenous and tribal peoples before permitting or undertaking exploration or exploitation. Indigenous and tribal peoples shall participate wherever possible in the benefits and shall receive "fair compensation" for damages.

Convention No. 107 provides much weaker protection of indigenous and tribal rights regarding land, resources and environment. Article 11, however, does provide that "[t]he right of ownership, collective or individual, of the members of the populations concerned over the lands which these populations traditionally occupy shall be recognized." Article 12 of the convention includes some requirements with respect to compensation for resettlement.

The meaning of these agreements has been clarified through the systems of the ILO for monitoring and enforcement of its conventions. Parties to a convention submit reports every five years regarding their compliance. A Committee of Experts on the Application of Conventions and Recommendations meets yearly to review and make comments on all reports submitted. The Committee may also make requests to governments for further information. Members of the ILO, which include employees' and employers' associations as well as governments, may also submit information to the Committee. While indigenous groups cannot directly lodge complaints, they may submit information indirectly through ILO members, such as employees' associations, from their countries. The Committee makes requests to governments concerning improved compliance, and publishes comments on reports, which can influence a government's compliance with its legal obligations. ILO also has technical assistance programmes relating to the two conventions.[27]

These conventions are not within the mainstream subject-matter of the ILO. They evolved within the ILO because of political needs for which there was not an ideal home. Yet although ILO Convention No. 169 is ratified by relatively few countries, it is significant as the leading instrument on indigenous peoples in international law. The Asian Development Bank includes it as an annex to its policy statements. The Inter-American Development Bank and World Bank refer to it in their policies on indigenous peoples. Preliminary findings from a study of Latin American judicial decisions suggest that courts in the region refer to it frequently, sometimes even in countries that have not ratified it.[28] The extent to which ILO Convention No. 169 gains influence will depend on the extent to which constituencies build domestic pressure in additional countries for ratification.[29] Because of the close association of indigenous and tribal peoples with forests, ILO Convention No. 169 has the potential to strengthen the human rights dimension of the international legal framework for forests. Its provisions provide a significant reference point in international law for protection of indigenous and tribal peoples' rights relating to forests, forest lands, and forest resources.

2. UN Working Group on Indigenous Populations

The UN Working Group on Indigenous Populations was established by the UN Economic and Social Council in 1982 under the Sub-Commission on Prevention of Discrimination and Protection of Minorities of the UN Commission on Human Rights. The Working Group has developed a Draft

---

[27] International Labour Office, *Recent Developments Concerning Indigenous and Tribal Peoples 1998*, Statement to the UN Working Group on Indigenous Populations (Geneva: ILO, 1998).

[28] Personal communication, Lee Swepston, Chief, Equality and Human Rights Coordination Branch, ILO, Geneva, 29 July 1998.

[29] While ILO members have no obligation to ratify, article 19 of the ILO Constitution requires them to "submit the Convention to the competent authorities" for consideration. Countries currently considering ratification of the convention are reported to include Argentina, Austria, Brazil, Chile, Finland, Philippines, and Venezuela.

United Nations Declaration on the Rights of Indigenous Peoples, which was adopted by the Sub-Commission in 1994.[30]

The Declaration, which covers a range of rights and freedoms, includes many provisions relevant to the relationship between indigenous peoples and forests. Perhaps the most important are those relating to indigenous lands and associated resources. For instance, Article 25 provides that "[i]ndigenous peoples have the right to maintain and strengthen their distinctive spiritual and material relationship with the lands, territories, ... and other resources which they have traditionally owned or otherwise occupied or used." Article 26 provides that "Indigenous peoples have the right to own, develop, control and use the lands and territories, including the total environment of the lands, ... flora and fauna and other resources which they have traditionally owned or otherwise occupied or used." Article 28 provides that "[i]ndigenous peoples have the right to the conservation, restoration and protection of the total environment and the productive capacity of their lands, territories and resources."

A preliminary review of publicly available information suggests that there are no significant programmes of UN activities specifically relating to indigenous rights and forests.[31] Further research might be helpful in that it could explore the extent to which any existing human rights programmes relate indirectly to forests. While not a programme, the Working Group's annual meetings, held since 1982, offer the opportunity for many governments, indigenous organizations, international organizations, NGOs, and scholars to convene to discuss a wide range of issues relating to indigenous peoples' concerns, and forests could be addressed in this context. It could be useful to research whether and how forests might have come up in past discussions. Research could involve review of documents produced at and for the meetings, together with interviews of selected officials and others familiar with the process.

If it were implemented by the world's governments, the Draft Declaration would have a profound impact on the relationships between indigenous peoples, non-indigenous peoples and forests. Yet significant obstacles stand in the way of the Declaration's implementation. Although the Sub-Commission has adopted it, the Commission on Human Rights has now established a separate working group that has begun rewriting its provisions. It is anticipated by some observers that this working group will weaken the Declaration's protections of indigenous rights.

As a public expression of the aspirations of the world's indigenous peoples, the Declaration is a milestone. Precisely because the Declaration expresses indigenous aspirations so well, it is currently considered unlikely that it will be adopted by higher-level UN organs in its present form, even as a non-binding instrument. Yet even if the Declaration were ultimately to be adopted by the UN General Assembly, it would be a non-binding instrument, imposing no legal obligations upon states that signed it. It could and should, however, serve a valuable function as a reference point for policies and laws on indigenous peoples developed in other forums ranging from multilateral development banks to the ITTO. Progress on the revision and adoption of the Declaration, and any aspects relevant to forests, should be monitored as part of future research in this area.

IV. International Trade and Investment Liberalization

One of the principal global instruments/institutions relating to the linkage between forests and trade is the World Trade Organization (WTO). A second is the Convention on International Trade in

---

[30] Available from UN human rights web site <http://www.unhchr.ch/hchr_un.htm>

[31] *See Technical Cooperation: Programme Focus*, available on United Nations Human Rights Website, at <http://www.unhchr.ch/html/menu2/4/prog.htm>.

Endangered Species (CITES). Both of these relate to all types of forests. A third global instrument, relevant only for tropical forests, is the International Tropical Timber Organization (ITTO), which administers the International Tropical Timber Agreement (ITTA), a commodity agreement between producers and consumers of tropical timber. The ITTO is examined in another chapter of this book.

In conjunction with discussion of the WTO, this section also reviews three other areas of recent activity that relate to the linkages between its trade rules and forests. The first involves investment liberalization, on which WTO discussions may begin in the coming few years, after the termination of talks at the OECD. The second involves ISO, which recently concluded discussions of the relationship between ISO technical standards and forest management; WTO rules recognise ISO's role in establishing international standards for traded products.

The third area involves the activities of the Forest Stewardship Council (FSC), which relates to forests and trade rules because the ecolabels that are certified by organizations accredited by FSC are sometimes applied to timber and timber products that move in international trade. Thus the discussion has arisen at the WTO as to whether such labels are consistent with WTO rules. Both ISO and FSC, in contrast to other institutions and instruments considered in this paper, are non-governmental.

The relationships between trade and forests are important because a significant minority of global timber products move in international trade. "Approximately one quarter of wood based panels and paper products and one fifth of sawnwood and wood pulp are traded internationally," while "6-7% of global industrial roundwood output is currently traded."[32] While only a fraction of timber and timber products are exported, exports are extremely important for some countries.[33]

Trade can have either negative or positive impacts on sustainable development and conservation of forests.[34] The export of timber, agricultural and wildlife products can intensify over-exploitation of forest wildlife and the conversion of forest habitat. By stimulating production, trade – ultimately driven by consumption in the importing country – can be an underlying cause of exploitation of forest species and conversion of forest ecosystems. At the same time, of course, export of forest products can provide income needed for development and poverty alleviation, if a significant proportion of the profits are returned to impoverished groups within a country.

The transportation and infrastructure involved in trade can also have significant effects, particularly through construction of roads, canals and pipelines through forestlands. On the one hand, this infrastructure can benefit forest communities by enhancing access to outside markets, improving communication, and increasing access to educational, health care and other resources. On the other hand, it can have severe impacts on forest ecosystems and resources important for local communities, and as a result there are numerous cases in which local forest communities oppose such projects. The importation of forest products can also result in the introduction of alien species,

---

[32] United Nations Department of Economic and Social Affairs (UNDESA), *Matters left pending on trade and environment*, at para. 7 (advance unedited text). Available at IFF web site <http://www.un.org/esa/sustdev/iff.htm>

[33] For instance, exports account for a majority of national commercial production in Indonesia, Malaysia, Papua New Guinea, and Congo. *See* Panayotis N. Varangis, Rachel Crossley and Carlos A. Primo Braga, *Is there a Commercial Case for Tropical Timber Certification*, at 18, POLICY RESEARCH WORKING PAPER 1479 (Washington: World Bank, 1995).

[34] This and the subsequent six paragraphs are adapted from David R. Downes, *Integrating Implementation of the Convention on Biological Diversity and the Rules of the World Trade Organization*, at 4 (Gland: IUCN, in press).

which can displace native species and destabilize ecosystems. Foreign direct investment (FDI) – trade in capital – is an increasingly important category of trade which often has significant impacts on forests, for instance through financing of infrastructure for export transportation (such as roads or pipelines) and investment in extractive industries.

Rules and policies for liberalization of trade and investment can intensify all these effects on forests by stimulating or facilitating new trade flows, expansion of existing flows, intensification of production techniques and expansion of productive capacity. In addition, the application of trade rules, as they have been interpreted to date, can interfere with national and possibly international conservation laws and policies – especially those which seek to control threats posed by trade or consumption of traded goods – thus magnifying the impacts of trade on forests. Already there have been several challenges to conservation laws under the General Agreement on Tariffs and Trade (GATT) and the WTO, such as the tuna/dolphin and shrimp/turtle cases. On the other hand, some trade rules, in particular disciplines on government subsidies to industry, could be applied so as to reduce impacts of production on forests.

The nature of the impact of commodity production on forests depends not only on the quantity of production but also the quality of the production or processing method (PPM). Producers choose among more or less environmentally friendly PPMs according to the prices for which products can be sold, the potential volume of sales, the availability and cost of needed know-how, capital, labour, and material resources. Producers' choice of PPM is also affected by incentives built into the economic system – including the international trading system – and the extent to which laws and policies – including trade rules – reward efforts at sustainability, require internalization of environmental costs, or forbid PPMs with environmental costs deemed excessive. If the laws and policies affecting consumption and production, including trade rules, effectively internalize costs and encourage transmission of information between producers and consumers about environmental impacts, then the result should be sustainable production and trade in products from biological resources such as forest ecosystems.

Another category of relationships, not examined in detail here, but which are potentially "positive", involve the trade in and use of forest genetic resources as a source of new products. Genetic resources – the foundation of all biodiversity – and associated chemicals found in diverse species are of increasing value as sources of new crop varieties, medicines, pesticides, biotechnological processes and other products. While the economic value of genetic resources is difficult to measure, the CBD establishes principles for benefit sharing and access that could promote greater economic returns to developing countries in whose territories biodiversity-rich tropical forests are found.

Negative trade-related impacts stem in part from principles of the world trade system combined with features of national law and policy frameworks. Under the economic theory underlying the world trading system, countries should specialize in production of products for which they have a comparative advantage in that their costs of production are lower. International trade rules reduce barriers to trade so that each country exports products for which it has a comparative advantage and imports products for which domestic production is more expensive. Global production is more efficient overall and every society benefits.

While this theory underlies a process of trade liberalization that has helped to spur increased production of many goods, critics argue that its application can also produce negative results for a country's economy and environment. Production of a primary commodity like timber inflicts significant environmental and social costs. Loss of forest cover often increases soil erosion, increases flooding, reduces water clarity which in turn harms fisheries, and reduces the supply of non-timber forest products important for local communities. If, however, the legal system does not regulate harvesting to control such "external" costs of production – for instance through the protection of property rights over the forest – then the private cost to the producer of harvesting the timber may be much lower than the total social cost of production.[35] That is, the logging company harvesting the timber does not have to pay for soil erosion, flooding, and other costs.

As a result, private gain from exports may produce net social loss in terms of overall forest values and productivity.[36] Liberalized trade may consequently intensify the social cost to the exporting country of its weak system of regulation. The result is "an *apparent* comparative advantage ... even where there is none," and "apparent gains from trade, which in reality could be losses."[37] As a result, "the world economy as a whole consumes an inefficient quantity of resources, because it takes no account of the costs to the world economy of the resource overuse."[38]

1. World Trade Organization ("WTO")

The World Trade Organization (WTO), formed in 1995, is intended to provide a regulatory and institutional framework for the world trading system.[39] It regulates national trade-related policies through a growing number of agreements that bind its 130-plus member countries. With the rapid growth in international trade, it has the potential to become one of the most powerful international organizations of the 21st century. The WTO was created under the Uruguay Round agreements, which were signed in Marrakesh in 1994. These agreements are binding upon all WTO members and in total are referred to here as the "WTO rules." The agreements and forums of the WTO discussed in this section include:

- the General Agreement on Tariffs and Trade (GATT); originally signed in 1947, this agreement was incorporated into the Uruguay Round agreements that bind WTO Members as the "GATT 1994";

- the Agreement on Technical Barriers to Trade (TBT Agreement);

- the Committee on Trade and Environment (CTE).[40]

1.1 The General Agreement on Tariffs and Trade (GATT).

The GATT's national treatment and most-favoured-nation obligations are basically non-discrimination rules. They forbid Members from treating foreign products less favourably (for example through higher taxes or more stringent regulation) than domestic "like products" or from treating products imported from one WTO member less favourably than "like products" from another

---

[35] *See* Graciela Chichilinsky, *North-South Trade and the Dynamics of Renewable Resources*, 4 STRUCTURAL CHANGE AND ECONOMIC DYNAMICS 219, 221 (1993).

[36] *See id,* at 222.

[37] *See* Graciela Chichilinsky, *Sustainable Development and North-South Trade* at 9 (paper prepared for University of Arizona conference, "Biological Diversity: Exploring the Complexities," Tucson, Arizona, 25-27 March 1994).

[38] *See id.*

[39] This discussion of the WTO is adapted from Downes, *Integrating Implementation, supra* n. 35.

[40] Also potentially relevant to forests are the Agreement on Trade Related Aspects of Intellectual Property (TRIPS Agreement), the Agreement on the Application of Sanitary and Phytosanitary Measures (SPS Agreement); the Agreement on Subsidies and Countervailing Measures (Subsidies Agreement); and the WTO Understanding on the Settlement of Disputes.

Member (Articles III and I). The term "like products" has been defined in past GATT and WTO dispute panel decisions to mean products with the same or similar physical characteristics or end uses. As a result, unilateral environmental trade measures that distinguish between products based on production or processing methods (PPMs) have been found in violation of these obligations. The GATT also prohibits most quantitative import and export restrictions on goods, such as quotas or bans (Article XI).

Article XX of the GATT, however, provides exceptions to these rules. Article XX(b) excepts measures necessary to protect human, animal, or plant life or health. Article XX(g) excepts measures relating to the conservation of exhaustible natural resources taken in conjunction with domestic restrictions. To qualify for these exceptions, a measure must also satisfy the requirements of the "chapeau" to Article XX. These requirements are that a measure shall not constitute arbitrary or unjustifiable discrimination between countries where the same conditions prevail and shall not constitute a disguised restriction on international trade.

1.2 The Agreement on Technical Barriers to Trade (TBT Agreement).[41]

The TBT Agreement is intended to ensure that WTO members do not use technical regulations and standards as disguised measures to protect domestic industries from foreign competition. It is also intended to reduce the extent to which technical regulations and standards operate as barriers to market access, primarily by encouraging their harmonization. Harmonization is expected to reduce the obstacles to international trade that can be created by the difficulty of complying with numerous, sometimes incompatible, standards and regulations in various countries.

The TBT Agreement creates different but related obligations for two defined categories of measures – regulations and standards. A "technical regulation" establishes mandatory require-ments for products or related processes and production methods (PPMs). A "standard," in contrast, establishes *voluntary* requirements for "products or related processes and production methods." Both regulations and standards may also relate to "terminology, symbols, packaging, marking or labelling requirements as they apply to a product, process or production method" (TBT Agreement, Annex I).

The TBT Agreement also applies indirectly to private and voluntary schemes through the Agreement's Code of Good Practice for the Preparation, Adoption and Application of Standards (the Code). Under the Code, a Member is obligated to "take such reasonable measures as may be available to [it]" to ensure compliance with the Code of private voluntary programmes within its territory, including its most-favoured nation and national treatment obligations.

The rules of the TBT Agreement, including its Code of Good Practice, prohibit both regulations and standards from discriminating between domestic products and foreign products that are alike (national treatment) and between "like" products from different WTO members ("most-favoured-nation").[42] Further, standards and regulations must not constitute unnecessary obstacles to trade, although if a regulation or standard is based upon an international standard, it

---

[41] Much of the discussion of the TBT agreement is drawn from David R. Downes and Brennan Van Dyke, *Fisheries Conservation and Trade Rules: Ensuring That Trade Law Promotes Sustainable Fisheries* at 13-14 (Washington: CIEL/Greenpeace, 1998).

[42] While the wording is slightly different, these obligations are substantially the same as those in the GATT.

is presumed not to create such an obstacle.[43] In addition, Members must ensure that central governmental standardizing bodies improve transparency and involve interested parties in standard setting; must take reasonable measures to ensure that regional standardization bodies of which they are members do the same; and must make reasonable efforts to harmonize technical rules at the international level.

The TBT Agreement does not contain an explicit environmental exception. Its preamble does, however, contain language paralleling that found in the environmental exception of Article XX of the GATT, recognizing that "no country should be prevented from taking measures necessary to ensure ... the protection of human, animal or plant life or health, [or] of the environment ... at the levels it considers appropriate."[44]

It is probable, although not entirely clear, that the TBT Agreement covers labelling standards concerning non-product related criteria, such as criteria related to process or production methods (PPMs).[45] Currently there is debate about whether and how the TBT Agreement's obligations might apply to ecolabelling initiatives. If the Agreement were interpreted to apply to ecolabelling initiatives in a way consistent with some past GATT decisions on trade and environment, they might be found inconsistent with its requirements. As a policy matter, some developing countries are concerned that ecolabelling could operate to foreclose market access for developing country producers less able to meet labelling and certification standards. Thus, it will be important to develop both ecolabelling initiatives and relevant interpretations of the TBT Agreement in ways that address concerns about market access while realizing the potential of this market tool for protecting forest ecosystems and resources.

1.3 The Committee on Trade and Environment (CTE)

The term of the CTE was extended at the May 1998 Ministerial Conference of the WTO. Its agenda, defined at the close of the Uruguay Round, includes a number of issues relevant to forests:

- the relationship between provisions of the multilateral trading system and trade measures under multilateral environmental agreements, e.g. CITES;

- the relationship between environmental policies relevant to trade and environmental measures with significant trade effects and trade rules;

---

[43] While the TBT Agreement does not designate any specific organization as competent to establish such international standards, other provisions of the Agreement refer repeatedly to ISO. As this suggests, the WTO appears to be comfortable with ISO as an international standardizing body, given its established role in trade- related harmonization efforts.

[44] This language goes beyond the language of Article XX(b) in that it refers explicitly to the environment. Article XX(b) has, however, been interpreted by GATT and WTO panels to encompass measures generally considered environmental within its language referring to measures "necessary to protect human, animal or plant life or health."

[45] The term non-product-related criteria refers to criteria that distinguish between products according to factors not related to the characteristics of the product itself. In the context of ecolabeling the most relevant non- product-related criteria are standards relating to the impacts on the environment or forests of production or processing methods (PPM). Another example of a non-product-related criteria would be a requirement that an imported good have been produced by the rightful owner of a relevant patent or a licensee of that patent holder – a requirement that in fact WTO Members are authorised to impose under Article 51 of the TRIPS Agreement.

- the relationship between trade rules and requirements for environmental purposes relating to products, including standards and technical regulations and labelling;

- the effect of environmental measures on market access, especially in relation to developing countries, in particular least developed countries; and

- the environmental benefits of removing trade restrictions and distortions.

WTO Members have made very little progress, however, toward resolving any of the issues on the CTE's agenda, including these.

1.4 Other WTO Bodies

As a result of this lack of progress, it is possible that Members will begin to address environmental issues within other specialized bodies in the context of specific agreements. In fact, the TBT Committee recently had discussions on forest product ecolabels. Thus far, however, these bodies have shown little inclination to take on the environmental problems that have stymied the CTE.

WTO Members have not yet succeeded in achieving resolution of trade and environmental concerns in any WTO deliberative body. The practical result is that the primary WTO forum for trade and environment issues has become its dispute resolution proceedings under the WTO Understanding on the Settlement of Disputes. This agreement establishes an elaborate mechanism for binding resolution of disputes according to WTO rules. The dispute settlement mechanism is intended to maintain a rules-based system to prevent trading nations from engaging in unconstrained use of economic power to impose protectionist, excessively burdensome, arbitrary or discriminatory measures on trading partners.

During the past two years, dispute panel decisions and appellate body decisions such as the US/Venezuela gasoline case have been practically the only multilateral mechanism that actually resolved any issues in the trade and environment debate. Recent examples include the appellate body decision affirming the US challenge to the EC bovine growth hormone ban and the appellate body decision affirming several Asian countries' challenge to the US ban on import of shrimp caught using trawl nets without turtle excluder devices. Other cases with environmental aspects are likely to arise.

A WTO dispute generally involves a small minority of Members and focuses on a specific trade-related measure. Dispute decisions also leave uncertainty about their impact on policy: technically, a decision in a dispute binds only the Members involved and does not control the outcomes of future disputes involving similar issues, although Members frequently look to the outcomes of disputes for guidance on how future disputes are likely to be decided. The WTO's current dispute settlement procedures are also closed to public scrutiny or input, although some governments have recently called for greater openness. The lack of transparency and lack of participation make these proceedings ill-suited venues for policy-making.

1.5 The WTO Overall

Many of the WTO's programmes relate to forests in indirect ways, as described above. The WTO does not, however, have a forest programme. In terms of human resources, the WTO has a sizable Secretariat in Geneva. A large number of countries keep permanent missions there, and many of them include trade experts on their delegations. Fewer of them, however, have environmental or forest expertise on staff. The Secretariat, too, has limited expertise of this kind available, although it has produced some useful preliminary analysis which should be reviewed more intensively in any future research in this area.[46] Decision makers in dispute proceedings are generally trade experts with relatively little background in other areas of law or policy. The WTO does not have significant financial resources to allocate to external programmes on forests or any other issue.

The WTO's focused mission on trade liberalization is probably both a strength and a weakness. The focus has allowed significant progress under the WTO and its predecessor, the GATT, allowing countries to enhance economic development through their comparative advantage in production of forest products. On the other hand, the WTO has had great difficulty in incorporating environmental and social concerns outside this narrow field of view. While the WTO has the potential to create indirect incentives for improved forest management, its inability so far to temper its free trade doctrine with adequate social and environmental safeguards makes it a possible threat to forests, and further analysis of its current and potential impacts on forests is needed. This research could include review of relevant documents, interviews with Secretariat staff, government delegates, non-governmental observers and commentators, and possibly economic and legal research.

2. Investment Liberalization[47]

As noted above, trends in foreign direct investment can have significant impacts on forests. The Agreement on Trade-Related Investment Measures (the TRIMS Agreement) concluded in the Uruguay Round imposes relatively weak obligations to liberalize investment. Hoping to strengthen these obligations, developed countries are now pressing to begin negotiations on an investment liberalization agreement within the WTO, and may well succeed in placing the issue on the agenda of the Millenial Round of WTO negotiations slated to begin in the year 2000. Already, developed countries had worked within the OECD to negotiate a Multilateral Agreement on Investment (MAI) that would be open for ratification by all countries. Recently, however, those negotiations ended. While not an immediate issue, the long term potential for investment liberalization to affect forest policy is profound. Thus, further research on the impact of global institutions and instruments on forests should include monitoring of future discussions on investment liberalization through periodic contacts with the WTO Secretariat, government delegations active on the issue, and non-governmental observers.

The draft MAI developed during the OECD talks illustrates how investment liberalization rules could affect forests. Proposed expropriation provisions, which provide for compensation when a company is deprived of its investment by a measure "tantamount to expropriation," could interfere with a government's efforts to manage and conserve forests within its national jurisdiction.

A recent case illustrates the potential for interference with sovereign control over environment and natural resources. In 1997 the Ethyl Corporation filed a US $250 million claim against the Canadian government, alleging violation of provisions under the North American Free Trade Agreement (NAFTA) that are similar to expropriation language included in the draft MAI. Ethyl challenged Canada's import ban on the toxic gasoline additive MMT, of which Ethyl was the leading supplier. The company argued that the regulation is equivalent to an expropriation of its investment. The Canadian government agreed in July 1998 to pay a reported US $13 million to

---

[46]   *See,* in particular, paragraphs 106-130 in World Trade Organization, Committee on Trade and Environment, *Environmental Benefits of Removing Trade Restrictions and Distortions: Note by the Secretariat* (Geneva: WTO, 1997). Doc. No. WT/CTE/W/67, 7 November 1997. Available on WTO Web site, <www.wto.org>.

[47]   This discussion of investment liberalization is drawn largely from Downes, *Integrating Implementation, supra* n. 35 at 14.

settle the case. Such challenges under a future agreement could inhibit the development, or force the roll back, of conservation regulations applied to the private sector to protect forests. In that case, as is typical for investment disputes, the proceeding was secret, with no right of access for the public, although the case involved significant public policy issues.[48]

3. ISO, the International Organization for Standardization[49]

ISO, the International Organization for Standardization, is an international federation of national standardization bodies from some one hundred countries, who work together to set standards for a wide range of goods and services. The ISO system is a series of industry wide standards that are designed to facilitate trading by establishing global standards for goods and services. Such standards are particularly useful in the exchange of goods where face to face transactions between buyer and seller are not possible because they provide assurance to the end purchaser that the ISO certified product will be suitable for their needs. Compliance with these standards is strictly voluntary. Participating producers volunteer to be inspected and certified by certification bodies. ISO does not monitor or accredit certification bodies. ISO is implicitly recognized as an international standardizing body important for the harmonization of standards for traded products through repeated references in the text of the TBT Agreement of the WTO.

Following the 1992 UNCE, and in response to growing international concern regarding industry's environmental impacts, ISO began developing a series of standards relating to the environment, the 14000 Environmental Management Standard series. The ISO 14000 standards seek to create general environmental management standards that an organization in any industry could draw upon to better manage its environmental impacts and risks. Within the ISO 14000 series is 14001, which provides for the establishment and certification of an environmental management system for participating organizations.

In 1995, the Standards Council of Canada and Standards Australia proposed that one of ISO's technical working groups (TC 207) develop standards for the application of ISO 14001 to the forestry sector. The proposal was withdrawn, in large part because it represented a deviation from the generic, non-sector specific nature originally agreed upon for the 14000 series.[50] Eventually, however, TC 207 agreed to create a technical report type III on the application of 14001 in forestry, the least binding level of documentation which is for information purposes only, does not provide guidance on compliance with the standard, and does not provide a basis for a possible future standard. In 1998, TC 207 ended its existence with production of that report.

Series 14000 certification is significantly different from an FSC accredited certification, discussed in Part III.D, below. If applied to a company's forest management system, ISO certification only verifies that the system is likely to meet the environmental goals set by the forest management company itself. Independent third party certification/auditing of the system is possible but not required. A forest company could be certified as compliant with ISO's standards for environmental management, yet apply any standard of forest management it chose, even if the result in the forest were clearly unsustainable. It is also notable that a company can obtain ISO certification even if its practices fail to comply with applicable environmental laws.

---

[48] Lawrence Herman, "*Expropriation takes on new meaning*," Financial Post, 28 July 1998, at 13.

[49] Some of this section is adapted from Gary Cook, David Downes, Brennan Van Dyke & John B. Weiner, *Applying Trade Rules to Timber Ecolabeling: A Review of Timber Ecolabeling and the WTO Agreement on Technical Barriers to Trade* 15 (Draft, CIEL 1997).

[50] Pierre Hauselmann, *Certification and Labeling of Forest Products: Complementarity Between Trade and Forest Policy* (Geneva: UNEP/IUCN, 1996).

Although some ISO standards, such as the 14000 series, could be applied to forest management, ISO currently has no programme focused on forests. Thus, it is difficult to speak of relevant
human and financial resources in this context. Future research on the international forest regime
should include monitoring of ISO, through periodic contacts with the organization and key
government delegations and non-governmental observers, in case ISO's activities become once
again more pertinent to forests.

4. Forest Stewardship Council

The Forest Stewardship Council (FSC) is unique among the institutions and instruments surveyed
here in that its mission relates explicitly and specifically to forests. It brings together environmental, social and economic interest groups to develop principles and criteria for responsibly managed
forests. The FSC promotes the implementation of such criteria through the certification of forest
products and production methods. The FSC accredits certifiers that comply with the FSC criteria;
those certifiers then certify producers. Producers certified by an FSC-accredited certifier can use
the FSC logo on their products. A significant number of such products move in international trade.
The FSC has been included in this section on trade because the relationship of ecolabelling with
international trade rules has become a hotly debated topic at the WTO and elsewhere. In particular,
there has been discussion of whether or how the ecolabels envisioned by the FSC are compatible
with the rules of the TBT Agreement of the WTO regarding voluntary standards for labelling of
products.

Founded in 1993, the FSC was developed outside of governmental and inter-governmental
frameworks. The FSC currently has 279 members from 40 countries. FSC members meet in
general assembly every three years and act as the final authority of the organization. Decisions are
made by an overall majority and the voting system seeks to ensure a balance between the three
chambers, consisting of social, environmental and economic interests, as well as between
developed and developing countries. A Secretariat, based in Oaxaca, Mexico, supports the FSC's
activities. Further research would be needed to determine the FSC's human and financial
resources, which could be carried out through means such as interviews with FSC officials.

The mandate of the FSC is based on the premise that consumers need reliable information
about the environmental and social impacts of forest-derived products in order to exercise their
market power to encourage methods of production that are environmentally and socially responsible. FSC believes that information about forest products and their production will be most reliable
if such information is provided by an independent, impartial certification process recognized by an
organization representing a wide range of interest groups. Currently, six certifiers have been
accredited by FSC, and they in turn have certified a total of 10,510,235 hectares of forest land,
accounting for an estimated 0.5% of global industrial production.[51]

By establishing national and regional working groups, the FSC has developed not only a set
of global principles and criteria identifying well-managed forests, but also is working toward the
development of a series of standards particular to individual forests and forest-dependent
communities. However, the percentage of world production certified by FSC accredited institutions is relatively small.

In light of this, some critics argue that after five years of existence the FSC is a failure. Some
industry critics also complain that FSC criteria and principles are "unrealistic" in that they are too
restrictive in comparison to industry practices. On the other hand, some environmentalists
complain that FSC criteria are too lenient to ensure the survival of forests.

---

[51] Information in this paragraph current as of 31 July 1998, from electronic message from James
Sullivan, Operations Director, FSC, 6 August 1998.

Although it has drawn criticism from all sides of the forest management debate, and has struggled to develop and maintain a workable structure for decision-making, some observers view the FSC as the most significant international process on SFM to date.[52] They argue that the FSC's progress should be measured not only in market share but also in broader influence. The existence of the FSC has arguably put pressure on governments to initiate their own national or collaborative efforts on SFM, helping to stimulate progress in the Montreal, Helsinki and other regional processes.[53] The FSC has also inspired other authorities to consider adoption of policies referring to or adapted from the FSC.[54] To date, the FSC's achievement – combining multi-stakeholder consultations, international coverage, performance criteria, and assurances of reliability through rigorous evaluation procedures and chain of custody requirements – is unique.

5. Convention on International Trade in Endangered Species of Wild Fauna and Flora (CITES)

The objective of the Convention on International Trade in Endangered Species of Wild Fauna and Flora (CITES) is to prevent the overutilization of species, subspecies, and populations (referred to collectively here as "species") due to international trade. To determine if a species should be protected, the parties evaluate biological and trade data pertaining to a species at periodic meetings of the Conference of the Parties (COPs).

If the parties determine that a species is threatened with extinction, and is or may be affected by trade, they may list the species in Appendix I which prohibits commercial trade in that species. If the parties determine that a species may become threatened unless international trade is regulated, they may list the species in Appendix II.

CITES prohibits commercial trade in species listed in Appendix I. Commercial trade in species listed under Appendix II is permitted if the exporting country determines that the export will not be detrimental to the survival of that species and issues an export permit.

In addition, a party may unilaterally include a species in Appendix III. An Appendix III listing requires the listing party to issue export permits for the species, and obligates importing countries to require presentation of export permits when the specimen comes from the listing party, and a certificate of origin when the specimen comes from another range state.

Approximately 800 species are listed on Appendix I and nearly 35,000 species are on Appendix II. While most parties are bound by such listings, a party may, however, make reservations to specific species when it becomes a party to CITES or at the time a species is listed. A party with a reservation is considered a non-party with respect to trade in that species.

To enforce their obligations, the parties must issue permits to ensure compliance with the appropriate scientific and management procedures for each shipment of a "specimen."[55] Before

---

[52] *See* William E. Mankin, *Entering the Fray: International Forest Policy Processes: An NGO perspective on their effectiveness*, London: IIED, in press. Policy that Works for Forests and People Series No. 9; *see also* Oliver DuBois, Nick Robins and Stephen Bass, *Forest Certification: A report to the European Commission*, at 61 (London: International Institute for Environment and Development, 1996) (citing the FSC as "highly significant").

[53] *See id.*

[54] *See id.*

[55] A specimen is defined as any readily recognizable part or derivative of a listed species.

issuing an import permit for an Appendix I specimen, the importing country must determine that the shipment is not for commercial purposes. Import permits are not required for Appendix II specimens. Before issuing an export permit for a specimen listed in Appendix I or II, the exporting country must certify that the shipment is not detrimental to the survival of the species. This is known as the "no-detriment" finding or requirement. The "no-detriment" requirement provides a rough estimate regarding the sustainability of trade. The Scientific Authority must also ensure that all exports of Appendix II specimens are limited in order to maintain that species throughout its range at a level consistent with its role in the ecosystems and above a level at which that species might become eligible for Appendix I.

By strictly regulating trade in species and, at the same time, creating opportunities for trade, the parties to CITIES have sought to balance ecological and economic concerns and thus ensure the sustainable management of species affected by trade.[56]

CITES was signed in 1973 and entered into force on July 1, 1975. It currently has 143 signatories. As mentioned, the Parties meet periodically in COPs to make decisions about listing and other aspects of implementation. A Secretariat assists the Parties with implementation by preparing relevant reports, recommending actions and policies for more effective implementation of CITES, organizing COPs and other meetings, and performing other tasks assigned by the Parties. Four permanent committees – the Animals, Plants, Identification Manuals, and Nomenclature Committees – assist the Parties with technical issues. The Standing Committee provides general policy and operational direction to the Secretariat and conducts other activities delegated by the Parties.

5.1 CITES and the Timber Trade

CITES applies to plant, just as it applies to animal, species. However, proposals to list endangered tree species, particularly species which are commercially harvested for their timber, are highly controversial. To date, the parties have listed only a few tree species.[57] Some of these are commercially important, such as the Brazilian Rosewood (*Dalbergia nigra*), listed in Appendix I, and the African Teak (*Pericopsis elata*), listed in Appendix II. Some mahoganies are also included

---

[56] While it does not involve a forest species, the case of the vicuña is a good example of the use of CITES, combined with national law and community development, to protect an endangered species and help local people gain benefits from sustainable use. The vicuña is highly prized for its very fine wool, and its numbers were greatly reduced by hunting in its native range in the Andes in South America. In 1975, international trade was banned under the Convention on International Trade in Endangered Species. Under national law in Peru and other Andean countries, hunting was prohibited, although some poaching continued. However, some local communities began to gather the animals seasonally and shear their wool. They processed the wool locally and then exported the cloth, carefully labeled to show that it came from sustainable harvesting. Consistent with this, CITES amended the trade ban to allow exports of properly labeled cloth from specific populations that were sustainably managed in Peru, Chile, Bolivia and Argentina. Local communities enjoying profits from the sale of the processed wool now have incentives to prevent poaching. While there are recent concerns that poaching may be on the increase again, over the course of the past 20 years this is a good example of the successful use of national and international law, combined with local action, to conserve a biological resource. Similar efforts may be possible for forest species.

[57] Seven species are listed on Appendix I, thirteen on Appendix II, and four on Appendix III. FAO, *State of the World's Forests 1997*, (Rome: FAO, 1997), *cited in* UNDPCSD, *Background Document Information on Trade and Environment*, Table 7 (New York: UNDPCSD, 1998).

in the Appendices, such as Pacific Coast Mahogany (*Swietenia humilis*) and Caribbean Mahogany (*S. mahagoni*), both included in Appendix II. Costa Rica and Bolivia have placed their populations of Bigleaf Mahogany (*S. macrophylla*) in Appendix III, and other range states, including Brazil and Mexico, have pledged to do the same.[58]

One way in which Parties have attempted to address the technical peculiarities of the timber trade has been to define the scope of listings to cover a manageable category of specimen types. For example, the listing for *Swietenia mahagoni* applies only to logs, sawn wood, and veneer sheets, and not to other parts or derivatives such as finished products. The Appendix I listing for *Pericopsis elata* applies to all specimens, however.

Many Parties seem reluctant to list timber-producing species in the Appendices for a variety of reasons. One involves the practical and technical problems that derive from incongruities between timber transport practices and CITES permit requirements. Another stems from the fact that some timber products, such as chemical extracts, are not readily recognizable specimens of the species.[59]

Parties also disagree over the role that CITES should play in issues affecting timber harvests and the timber trade. Some Parties believe that the CITES permit system unduly interferes with the commercial viability of the trade. Some Parties and trade interests also seem to mistakenly believe that all trade in Appendix II species is prohibited.[60] Dissension also occurs during debates regarding the basis upon which scientific evidence pertaining to the listing of a timber species. For example, the Plants Committee and the Secretariat, which make recommendations based upon scientific evidence, have recommended at previous COPs that the Parties place *Swietenia macrophylla* in Appendix II. Yet, the Parties, after intense debate, rejected the proposals, by six votes at COP9 and eight at COP10.

5.2 The Timber Working Group

In response to this controversy, the Parties created the Timber Working Group (TWG) at COP9. The TWG included balanced representation from boreal, temperate and tropical forest States, developed and developing countries, timber-producing and timber-importing States, intergovernmental organizations (such as the ITTO) and non-governmental organizations.

The TWG sought to identify implementation problems, clarify the meaning of "readily recognizable" parts and derivatives as it relates to trade in timber products, and examine the role of CITES vis-à-vis other international organizations. Of great importance, the TWG helped inform members about the specific implications of CITES for the timber trade, and to clarify CITES's implications for those more familiar with the timber trade and less familiar with CITES. The Parties adopted all of the TWG's recommendations at COP10.

---

[58] Donald Barry, United States Fish and Wildlife Service, Testimony before U.S. House of Representatives Committee on Resources Regarding the Results of the 10th COP of CITES, July 17, 1997, available through U.S. Fish and Wildlife Service web site at <http://www.fws.gov>

[59] Thus, the Parties have listed only certain types of specimens of some species. For the yew tree, or *Taxus wallichiana*, from which taxol is extracted, the listing excludes end-product medicines and chemical extracts from trade controls.

[60] In fact, it appears that some developers have stopped using materials derived from Appendix II listed species for this reason. See *Increasing Public Understanding of the Role of the Convention in the Conservation of Timber Species*, Recommendation of the Second Meeting of the Timber Working Group of CITES, CITES Doc. SC.37.13, TWG.02.Concl.09 (Rev.3) (1996).

The TWG identified a number of ways to adjust CITES requirements to accommodate the special needs of the timber trade while at the same time conforming to the conservation objectives of CITES. For example, the TWG discovered that many timber traders store shipments of timber in bonded warehouses for more than six months before selling the timber. Because export permits pursuant to CITES are only valid for six months, the TWG recommended a six month extension for export permits for timber products, but only if the shipments of timber arrive at the designated port of final destination and are held in Customs bond.

The TWG also resolved a few practical problems that may improve monitoring and identification of timber species in trade. For example, the TWG harmonized the definitions of "logs," "sawn wood," and "veneer sheets," with those of the Harmonized System of the World Customs Organization. To simplify reporting, TWG created universal terms for the reporting of exports and imports which will make permitting easier, and recommended uniform units of measurement for various categories of timber products.

5.3 Current Status and Next Steps

CITES offers significant institutional capacity and human resources for addressing the mixed trade and conservation concerns involved in managing the impact of trade on forest species. The Secretariat, COPs and various committees and working groups provide a structure for continuing discussion, information exchange and decision-making among Parties. All Parties must designate management authorities and scientific authorities responsible for implementation of CITES. After more than three decades of experience, many of these agencies have developed substantial expertise to contribute to problem solving.

CITES does not include provisions for mechanisms to finance implementation. A number of developed country Parties have, however, provided significant amounts of bilateral assistance to developing country Parties. Some species listings are also designed to encourage the return of economic benefits to the exporting country and in some cases source communities within the country, in theory providing a form of financing for implementation.

The TWG illustrates efforts to respond flexibly and practically to complex implementation issues relating to forest products, and illustrates the contribution CITES makes in the international efforts to conserve and sustainably manage timber-producing species. The success of the TWG to date suggests that the Parties might consider establishing a permanent timber working group or species-specific working groups to examine trade patterns, identify threats to timber species, identify appropriate levels of trade, and determine the best means for deciding what constitutes "no-detriment" for particular species.[61]

In fact, a new Mahogany Working Group is addressing issues specifically relating to the trade in and biology of *Swietenia macrophylla* and this group may provide valuable insight into methods for CITES regulation of a single species. The working group was scheduled to produce a report at the end of 1998 that makes recommendations for improving sustainability of trade-related harvesting.

---

[61] The TWG did recommend that the COP continue the working group through the next COP, and the COP, as already noted, adopted all of the working group's recommendations.

V. Climate Change

Scientific evidence suggests that anthropogenic (human-caused) emissions of greenhouse gases (GHGs) – gases which trap the radiation from the Earth's surface in the atmosphere – will result in global climate change. The Intergovernmental Panel on Climate Change (IPCC), an international panel of government-designated scientific experts, predicts that greenhouse gas emissions could result in an increase in global average temperature of 1-3.5 °C by the year 2100.[62] The IPCC estimates that this level of climate change will cause a 15 to 95 cm rise in sea level, an increased occurrence of extreme weather patterns, and disruption of hydrologic cycles and oceanic currents. Isotherms are anticipated to shift poleward 150 to 550 kilometres over the next 100 years.[63] The alteration of climate would also result in more frequent outbreaks of pests and pathogens as well as more frequent and intense forest fires.[64]

Global warming, if not mitigated, will have an injurious impact on forests in many regions of the world over the course of the next century. An average global temperature increase of as little as 1 °C would be sufficient to disturb local climate regimes to the effect that the growth and regeneration capacity of forests would be adversely affected. According to the IPCC, increased temperatures and the reduced availability of water will cause one-third of existing forests to experience dramatic changes in vegetation. While new ecosystems would surely emerge, such a drastic and rapid transformation will likely cause many species of trees and wildlife to be extinguished.

1. Carbon Sinks and Forest Management

Carbon dioxide (CO_2) is the most abundant contributor to the GHGs which produce climate change; it is released into the atmosphere by the burning of fossil fuels and forests. Through the process of photosynthesis, trees absorb or "sequester" atmospheric carbon in their roots and branches and thereby serve as natural "carbon sinks," while forest soils and other forest vegetation also sequester carbon. By sequestering more carbon than they release, natural forests can reduce the concentration of CO_2 in the atmosphere and lower a country's net emissions of GHGs. Forests currently cover 3.4 billion hectares of the Earth's surface.[65] Thus, international forest policy and forest management are essential to the issues surrounding the climate change crisis.

Much scientific and technical work remains to be done to establish generally accepted methodologies and definitions for measuring the carbon fluxes generated by different types of forest management in different types of forests. Standardization is essential for such matters as organizing and maintaining an inventory system to measure progress toward the emissions reduction commitments set forth in the Kyoto Protocol to the Framework Convention on Climate Change (FCCC) adopted in December 1997.

---

[62] Intergovernmental Panel on Climate Change (IPCC). 1995. Summary for Policymakers: The Science of Climate Change - IPCC Working Group I. <http://www.ipcc.ch/>

[63] An isotherm in this context is "a line on a map connecting points on the Earth's surface having the same mean temperature." Webster's New World Dictionary of the American Language at 749 (2d college edition, New York: Simon & Schuster, 1982).

[64] IPCC, *Climate Change 1995: Impacts, Adaptations and Mitigation of Climate Change: Scientific and Technical Analyses*, Ed. Robert T. Watson, et al, at 115-116, 118, 121 (1996).

[65] IPCC. *Technologies, Policies and Measures for Mitigating Climate Change.* Ed. Watson, Robert T., Marufu C. Zinyowera, and Richard H. Moss, at 55 (1996) [hereinafter IPCC, *Mitigating Climate Change*].

2. The United Nations Framework Convention on Climate Change (FCCC)

The United Nations Framework Convention on Climate Change (FCCC)[66] was adopted in Rio at the United Nations Conference on the Environment and Development (UNCED) in 1992. The objective of the Convention is to achieve "stabilization of greenhouse gas concentrations in the atmosphere at a level that would prevent dangerous anthropogenic interference with the climate system."

The FCCC requires Parties to submit reports on national carbon inventories, sources of emissions, removal of sinks, and descriptions of national policies enacted to mitigate climate change.[67] The FCCC mandates an accounting of national inventories of carbon sources and sinks. It does not, however, establish a generally acceptable method for measuring carbon inventories. The IPCC's 1996 Revised Guidelines for assessing land-use change and forestry included methodologies for assessing carbon in aboveground biomass and in the soil, but did not address many issues, such as accounting for the carbon in subsurface biomass, wood products, and landfills.[68]

To remedy these and other shortcomings, the June 1998 meeting of the Subsidiary Body of Scientific and Technical Advice (SBSTA) asked the IPCC to prepare a Special Report on Land-Use, Land-Use Change and Forestry and Carbon Emissions. The report is intended to review the scientific and technical issues relating to carbon storage and emissions. It will also explore the potential for national GHG inventories, project-based accounting, monitoring and verification procedures. The report is due in the Spring of 2000.

The FCCC entered into force in 1994. As of January 28, 1998, the Convention was ratified by 174 countries. The FCCC Secretariat collects and analyses information and organizes frequent meetings such as those of the Conference of the Parties (COP), the SBSTA, and the Subsidiary Body on Implementation (SBI). The FCCC Secretariat is servicing discussions on the Kyoto Protocol as well, and the FCCC COPs serve as meetings of the signatories of the Kyoto Protocol.

3. The Kyoto Protocol

In December 1997, the COP adopted the Kyoto Protocol[69] to the FCCC, which establishes targets and schedules for reductions of net greenhouse gas emissions in the "Annex I" countries – developed countries and countries with economies in transition.[70] Forests are relevant to meeting

---

[66] United Nations Framework Convention on Climate Change, 29 May 1992, 31 I.L.M. 894 (1994).

[67] Article 12.1(a).

[68] FCCC Subsidiary Body for Scientific and Technological Advice. Eighth session. (1998). FCCC/SBSTA/1998/INF.1 *Methodological Issues; Issues Related to Land-use Change and Forestry.* <http://www.unfccc.de> "Belowground biomass" is carbon that is stored in living organisms or their parts found in the soil, such as microbes, invertebrates, and roots.

[69] Kyoto Protocol to the United Nations Framework Convention on Climate Change, December 10, 1997, FCCC/CP/1.7/Add.1.

[70] Article 3 requires Parties listed on Annex I of the FCCC to achieve a specified percentage of their 1990 levels by 2008-2012, as defined in Annex B to the Protocol. Annex B provides that three Parties are allowed to increase their net carbon emissions from 1990 levels, three Parties must maintain the same 1990 levels, and the rest must achieve reductions ranging from 5 to 8 percent.

these obligations under article 3, which provides that "[t]he net changes in greenhouse gas emissions from sources and removals by sinks resulting from direct human-induced land-use change and forestry activities, limited to afforestation, reforestation and deforestation since 1990 ... shall be used to meet the commitments under this Article."

However, the interpretation of the terms "afforestation, reforestation and deforestation" is highly controversial and decisions about their definition will have significant implications for both the Protocol's goals and the status of forests. The definition of "deforestation" is critically important, since only those forms of logging equivalent to deforestation will count against a country in its inventory of carbon fluxes. Likewise, there are concerns that "afforestation"[71] and "reforestation"[72] could be interpreted to allow countries to avoid counting of emissions under the Protocol, or even receive credit for sequestration, by simply replanting homogenous tracks of young trees in lieu of promoting sustainable management of old-growth forests.

The Protocol provides three mechanisms for interaction among Parties in the implementation of the Protocol: joint implementation, emissions trading, and the clean development mechanism. Each of these has potential significance for forests. The project-based mechanisms, JI and the CDM, are most relevant.

— **Joint Implementation**. Article 6 provides for joint implementation (JI), which allows an Annex I country to receive credit toward its emissions reduction commitment through financing of reductions in carbon emissions or enhancements of sinks in another Annex I country. The object of JI is to increase efficiency in the achievement of commitments where net reductions in the second country are cheaper than those in the first country. JI projects are most likely to be carried out in countries with economies in transition. Although most of the projects initiated pursuant to Article 6 will probably be in the energy sector, some countries with economies in transition, especially Russia, have large forests under threat of deforestation which would qualify them as candidates for JI projects.

— **Emissions Trading**. Article 17 provides that the Parties shall "define the relevant principles, modalities, rules and guidelines ... for emissions trading" among "Annex B" (equivalent to Annex I) countries. The emissions trading system envisaged under Article

---

[71] The IPCC defines afforestation as "planting of new forests on lands which historically have not contained forests." This language does not specifically forbid the sacrifice of non-forestlands, with their biodiversity and other ecological values, to plant a monoculture plantation. Further, land used for commercial plantations might usurp land required for domestic agriculture, and therefore increase the pressure to clear forest. Thus, it will be important to ensure that implementation of the Kyoto Protocol is consistent with other international agreements such as the Biodiversity Convention and that it does not encourage, directly or indirectly, conversion of habitat important for the conservation of biodiversity and sustainable use of biological resources.

[72] The IPCC defines "reforestation" as "planting of forests on lands which, historically, previously contained forests, but which have been converted to some other use." The FAO omits reference to an intervening land-use change in its definition of "reforestation;" rather FAO counts the natural or enhanced regeneration of biomass immediately following harvest as reforestation. Because the practice of planting directly after clear-cutting is common in temperate and boreal forests, Annex I Parties seeking to maximize credit toward emissions reduction targets may attempt to employ the FAO rather than the IPCC definition. If successful, such an outcome would be problematic from a sustainable management standpoint since it would eliminate or reduce the penalty suffered by Annex I countries resulting from deforesting activities by allowing them to credit their emissions with the carbon sequestration resulting from their so-called "reforestation."

17 would allow Annex B countries that could efficiently reduce emissions below target levels to sell their remaining "assigned amount" to other Annex B countries that are having trouble performing their emissions reduction obligations. It is not clear whether or how emissions trading might relate to forests.

— **Clean Development Mechanism (CDM)**. Article 12 establishes the clean development mechanism (CDM) under which Annex I countries can receive credits toward their reduction commitments by supporting mitigation activities in developing countries. The clean development mechanism is intended to "assist Parties not included in Annex I in achieving sustainable development and in contributing to the ultimate objective of the Convention, and to assist Parties included in Annex I in achieving compliance with their quantified emissions limitation and reduction commitments under Article 3."

Whether the CDM should include projects in which an Annex I country finances sequestration of carbon in forests in a developing country is controversial. As a matter of interpretation, it is unclear whether the negotiators intended to include carbon sequestration projects at all, since the language of Article 12 refers only to emissions "limitation and reduction" commitments. As a matter of policy, some countries are concerned about the sovereignty implications of allowing outside investors to finance and hence to some extent control management of significant areas of domestic forests. There are also concerns about the diversion of attention from the primary responsibility of developed countries, which have produced by far the bulk of GHGs to date, to reduce emissions and shift away from fossil fuel based technology. Furthermore, there are concerns that the CDM's rules must be designed to ensure that not only carbon values but other values such as biodiversity are protected in all projects.

However, the design of CDM projects and a system for promoting and monitoring them raises complex and difficult verification and methodological issues. An initial problem is to ascertain a baseline against which project effects can be measured. To some extent, defining the baseline must rely on historical deforestation trends. Yet baselines must also take into account a range of changing economic and other factors, including the impacts of the project itself.[73]

Another problem is generally termed "leakage," the "unexpected loss of estimated net carbon sequestered" which occurs when the project at hand causes carbon emissions to increase off the project site.[74] Leakage through activity-shifting occurs when the forest adjacent to the project is degraded or lost because the root causes of deforestation, such as need for agricultural land, have not been addressed, so the activities affecting forests are simply displaced to nearby parcels of land. Leakage must be addressed by designing projects and the policy frameworks that support them to respond to underlying causes – such as local communities not receiving adequate benefits from forest use.[75]

Countries must address these problems and others through the design of a strong set of rules for the CDM if climate change and threats to forests are to be addressed effectively. As summed up by an independent analysis of the implications for the CDM of pilot JI projects,

---

[73] Donald Goldberg, *Carbon Conservation: Climate Change, Forests and the Clean Development Mechanism* at 6 (Washington, D.C.: Center for International Environmental Law, CEDARENA, 1998).

[74] Paige Brown, Bruce Cabarle and Robert Livernash, *Carbon Counts: Estimating Climate Change Mitigation in Forestry Projects* 5 (World Resources Institute 1997).

[75] *See id*, at 8. In addition, it is important to design the project with large enough geographical boundaries to encompass the interrelated impacts on adjacent forestlands. *See* Goldberg, *Carbon Conservation, supra* n. 74, at 8.

given the right legal institutional framework, CDM forest projects could be potent tools in achieving climate benefits while protecting forests and benefiting local communities .... [However,] [i]f the legal and institutional framework for the CDM is not carefully designed, with both climate and other environmental and social impacts considered, the resulting investments and incentives could undermine both forest conservation and climate change goals.[76]

The technical resources available through the FCCC and Kyoto instruments include the Secretariat staff and the government officials regularly designated for the COP, SBSTA and SBI. The IPCC offers formidable technical and scientific resources – a cross section of the relevant scientific expertise in the world today. Financial resources for developing country implementation are available under the GEF (further discussed in another chapter in this volume), which is currently the financial mechanism for the FCCC. Additional financing may become available under the CDM, depending on whether and how forest projects are included within its scope. Further research and analysis is needed of the strengths and weaknesses of these institutions, which could involve review of documents produced in the relevant international processes, non-governmental commentary and analysis, and interviews with selected officials of the Secretariat, government delegations and non-governmental observers.

VI. Desertification

Desertification and drought are both phenomena which can adversely affect forests in many parts of the world. It is estimated that 250 million people are directly affected by desertification, while one billion people are at risk.[77] In addition, some 70% of the world's drylands (3,600 million hectares) are considered degraded.[78]

The main causes are climactic fluctuations and unsustainable land use, including deforestation. At the same time, however, forests can help to stabilize soils, mitigating against desertification and drought. Thus in arid, semi-arid and dry sub-humid regions of the Earth, factors affecting desertification and drought are also related to deforestation.

Because of the complex causes of desertification and drought, the IPF concluded the following:

Forest-related action aimed at combating desertification and mitigating the effects of drought should address the causes of those phenomena in an integrated manner, and should consider the role of poverty along with land use policies, food security, the provision of fodder and fuelwood, the effects of non-sustainable production and consumption patterns, the impact of trade and trade relations, migration, refugees and many other economic, social and cultural factors.[79]

Forest fires too were identified as possibly having devastating effects on such fragile ecosystems. Because of these multiple and complex factors, the Panel called for an integrated policy framework which combines bottom-up with top-down approaches.

---

[76] *See* Goldberg, n. 74, at 1.

[77] Interim Secretariat for the Convention to Combat Desertification, *An Introduction to the United Nations Convention to Combat Desertification*, 1997.

[78] Interim Secretariat for the Convention to Combat Desertification, *The Causes of Desertification*, 1997.

[79] IPF Final Report, paragraph 42.

The conclusion of the UN Convention to Combat Desertification in Those Countries Experiencing Serious Drought and/or Desertification, Particularly in Africa (hereinafter "Desertification Convention"), in 1994 was the culmination of a negotiating process that began at UNCED. The objective is to be achieved through effective action at all levels, in the framework of an integrated approach and the achievement of sustainable development in affected areas. This integrated approach involves addressing the physical, biological and socio-economic aspects of the processes of desertification and drought.[80] The holistic approach of the Convention can be illustrated by the definition provided of land degradation: as reduction or loss, in arid, semi-arid and dry sub-humid areas, of the biological or economic productivity and complexity of certain land resulting from land uses or processes such as long-term loss of vegetation.[81]

Affected country Parties undertake to

- give due priority to combating desertification and mitigating the effects of drought;

- establish strategies and priorities to combat desertification and mitigate the effects of drought;

- address the underlying causes of desertification;

- promote awareness and facilitate participation of local populations in efforts to combat desertification and mitigate the effects of drought; and

- provide an enabling environment through legislation, policies and action programmes.[82]

Affected country Parties are to prepare national action programmes, as appropriate in the framework of the regional implementation annexes, which should be updated regularly and be closely inter-linked with other policies for sustainable development.[83] National Action Programmes are to identify the factors contributing to desertification and the practical measures necessary to combat desertification and mitigate the effects of drought.[84] In so doing, they shall specify the roles of government, local communities and land users, and shall, *inter alia*, give particular attention to implementing preventive measures for land not yet or only slightly degraded, promote policies and strengthen institutional frameworks, and provide for effective participation.[85] The Convention also requires affected country Parties to consult and prepare sub-regional and regional action programmes.[86] Support is to be given for the elaboration and implementation of action programmes, including financial co-operation.[87] Requirements relating to information collection, analysis, and exchange,[88] as well as research and development,[89] are also set forth. The Convention also requires that Parties prepare national reports on the implementation of the Convention.[90]

---

[80] Article 4(2)(a).

[81] Article 1(f).

[82] Article 5.

[83] Article 9(1).

[84] Article 19(1).

[85] Article 10(2).

[86] Article 11.

[87] Article 13.

[88] Article 16.

[89] Article 17.

[90] Article 26.

The Convention contains a set of regional implementation annexes, which contain more specific obligations. The ones for Africa and Latin America and the Caribbean require national action programmes to integrate and sustainably manage natural resources, including forests.[91]

The Convention, which entered into force on 26 December 1996, is still in the early phase of implementation. Already some implementation activities reported involve agro-forestry, although the build of the work being done at this stage is organisational and procedural.[92]

Therefore, future analyses of the international forest regime will need to monitor the development of this instrument. One area to closely monitor concerns traditional knowledge, which is to be protected, promoted, and used.[93] The survey done by the Secretariat for COP-2 on this topic contains several provisions relating to forests.[94] A second key area concerns synergies with other international environmental treaties. The Parties have already expressed synergy as an important goal for the Convention, and a report prepared by the Secretariat emphasises that vegetation conservation is an important thread through the Desertification, Biological Diversity and Climate Change conventions.[95] Specifically, the report suggested potential areas of synergy include capacity building, scientific and technical cooperation, financial cooperation, and preparation of national strategies. Regarding the latter, future research should focus particularly on country-level impacts.

---

[91] Article 8(3)(b)(i) for Africa and Article 4(c) for Latin America and the Caribbean.

[92] *See*, e.g. Note by the Secretariat, Review of the Implementation of the Convention and of its Institutional Arrangements, Including Support to Regional Action Programmes, UN Doc. ICCD/COP(2)/5, 31 August 1998

[93] Article 18(2).

[94] Note du secretariat, Synthese des Rapports sur les Connaissances Traditionelles, UN Doc. ICCD/COP(2)/CST/5, 6 octobre 1998.

[95] Note by the secretariat, Promotion and Strengthening of Relationships With Other Relevant Convention: Collaboration and synergies among Rio conventions for the implementation of the UNCCD, UN Doc. ICCD/COP(2)/7, 17 November 1998.

Global Cooperation on Forests through International Institutions

By Richard G. Tarasofsky and David R. Downes

I. Introduction

This paper examines a selection of international institutions at the global level whose mandate and work programmes relate to the conservation, sustainable management and sustainable development of forests. Its methodology is similar to the chapter in this volume by David Downes, in that it seeks to identify the following:

- The mandate of each institution and its relationship to the conservation and sustainable management of forests;

- The forest and forestry-related programmes and the human and financial resources for these programmes;

- The strength and weakness of each institution with respect to matters such as the technical expertise of staff, financial resources, and political support for its mandate;

- The potential for future success and the identification of obstacles that might block progress on implementation of forest-related programmes or obligations.

As in the previous chapter, it must be noted that the examination here is not necessarily fully comprehensive.

II. Review of International Institutions

1. International Tropical Timber Organization

The International Tropical Timber Organization (ITTO) is primarily a commodity organization, which aims to regulate the international trade in tropical timber between producer and consumer countries. Membership in the ITTO at 50 members, including the European Community, is such that more than 90% of the world's tropical timber trade is covered, as are approximately 75% of the tropical rainforests. The International Tropical Timber Agreement (ITTA), which creates the ITTO, was originally adopted in 1983, under the auspices of UN Conference on Trade and Development (UNCTAD).

The ITTO's activities relate to policy development and projects. Its mandate is described by the IFF Secretariat as promoting trade in tropical timber, implementing the ITTA, promoting the conservation and sustainable management of tropical forests with a balance between conservation and utilization, and preventing deforestation in tropical forests.[1] It mission statement is as follows:

The ITTO facilitates discussion, consultation and international cooperation on issues relating to the international trade and utilization of tropical timber and the sustainable management of its resource base.

The ITTO is composed of the International Tropical Timber Council (ITTC), which is the governing body, and a small secretariat. The votes in the ITTC are equally split between producing and consuming countries, but within each bloc, individual country votes are allocated on the basis of market share. The ITTC has three Permanent Committees: Economic Information and Market

---

[1] IFF Secretariat, *Information on Forest-Related Work of International and Regional Organizations*, Background Document 4, New York, 1998.

Intelligence, Reforestation and Forest Management, and Forest Industry. It has a small secretariat, of 14 professionals in 1997, based in Yokahama, Japan.

The original ITTA objectives mainly related directly to trade, but also encouraged sustainable use and conservation of tropical forests.[2] It contained very little else of substance in relation to this latter objective, except providing for the possibility that projects on management were among those which the ITTO could undertake, and that forest management issues (mainly assessing and reviewing) was to be within the mandate of the Reforestation and Forest Management Committee. According to the ITTO, however, the

> underlying, though unstated, foundation of the Agreement lies in a two-way mutually supportive relationship between the tropical timber trade and conservation.[3]

In 1990, the Council adopted the Year 2000 Objective, which states exports of tropical timber should be from sustainably managed sources by the year 2000.[4] This Objective was adopted following a proposal made in the Committee on Forest Industry. In 1995, aware of the short time until 2000, the Council identified 7 priority actions as essential for achieving the Objective, relating to: adopting forest policy and applying legislation, securing the permanent forest estate, applying reduced impact logging, training the workforce, limiting harvest to sustained yield capacity, raising political and consumer awareness, focusing forest research on the analysis and using of existing data and knowledge.[5]

Because the original ITTA was due to expire in 1994, it was necessary to negotiate a successor agreement. After very acrimonious negotiations in 1993 and 1994 – with considerable controversy over whether the scope should be expanded to cover all timber trade – the ITTA 1994 was adopted. Ultimately, it was decided to retain the original scope of application, i.e. to tropical timber, but only after consumer countries made a formal statement which is attached to the Agreement, committing themselves to implement similar obligations relating to sustainable forest management for their forests as provided for in the Agreement. It entered into force on 1 January 1997.

The ITTA 1994 is more concrete than its predecessor in relation to conservation and management issues. Its objectives now include:[6]

- Contributing to the process of sustainable development;
- Enhancing the capacity of members to implement a strategy for achieving exports of tropical timber and timber products from sustainably managed sources by the year 2000;
- Promoting the expansion and diversification of international trade in tropical timber by improving the structural conditions in the market, including by having prices reflect the costs of sustainable forest management;
- Promoting and supporting research and development to improve forest management and efficiency of wood utilisation, as well as increasing the capacity to conserve and enhance other forest values;
- Developing and contributing to mechanisms to provide new and additional financial resources and expertise to enhance the capacity of members in achieving the objectives of the Agreement;

---

[2] Article 1.

[3] ITTO, *International Tropical Timber Organization – Ten Years of Progress*, p. 10.

[4] Decision 3(X).

[5] Annex B of Decision 8(XX)

[6] Article 1.

- Promoting increased processing of tropical timber from sustainable sources in producing member countries;
- Encouraging members to support and develop industrial tropical timber reforestation and forest management activities, as well as rehabilitation of degraded forest land, with due regard for the interests of dependant local communities;
- Improving marketing and distribution of tropical timber exports from sustainably managed sources;
- Encouraging members to develop national policies aimed at sustainable utilization and conservation of timber producing forests and their genetic resources and at maintaining the ecological balance in the regions concerned, in the context of timber trade;
- Promoting access to, and transfer of, technologies and technical cooperation to implement the objectives of the Agreement.

Unfortunately, the ITTA 1994 dilutes the original Year 2000 Objective (see the second bullet point above), although its creation of the Bali Partnership Fund to help members make the investments necessary to achieve the revised Objective may eventually be significant. In allocating the Fund, the Council is to take account of the special needs of members who are economically adversely affected by implementing the Year 2000 Objective and the needs of members with significant forest areas who establish conservation programmes in timber producing forests.[7] The Fund is not yet operational, which at this late date will clearly impact on the achievement of the Year 2000 Objective and it is also not certain what its actual resources will be, since it mainly depends on voluntary contributions.[8] But a decision was recently taken to begin identifying projects, pre-projects and activities eligible for funding.[9]

In addition to the Bali Partnership Fund, the ITTO has already funded over 300 projects covering each of its substantive areas referred to above. The funds for this come out of its Special Account, which is financed mainly by voluntary contributions. Japan is by far the greatest contributor.[10] In 1997, the Special Account included $18,137,365.51, down from $24,408,290.94 in 1996. Numerically, as well as financially, most pre-projects and projects relate to reforestation and forest management.

The ITTO has adopted a number of policy guidance documents. These include Guidelines on the Establishment and Sustainable Management of Planted Tropical Forests, Guidelines for the Sustainable Management of Natural Tropical Forests, Guidelines on the Conservation of Biological Diversity in Tropical Production Forests, Guidelines on Fire Management in Tropical Forests, and most recently, Criteria and Indicators for Sustainable Management of Tropical Forests (which replaces the 1991 Criteria for the Measurement of Sustainable Tropical Forest Management).

In 1998, the ITTO adopted the Libreville Action Plan (1998-2001), the second such action plan in its history. The expressed aim of this Action Plan is to take on board the substance of the renegotiated ITTA. The Goals of the Action Plan are grouped around the mandates of the ITTO Committees. The ones relating to Reforestation and Forest Management include: supporting

---

[7] Article 21(4).

[8] Article 21(2). Some commitments to the Bali Partnership Fund have already been made, mainly from Japan.

[9] Decision 8(XXV)

[10] In 1997, Japan contributed $13,600,468.23. Japan also provides the ITTO with office accommodations, facilities and equipment, as well as some seconded staff. It is also worth noting that Japan commands the greatest share of votes among the consumer countries.

activities to secure the tropical timber resources base, improving the tropical timber base, and enhancing technical, financial and human capacities to manage the tropical timber base. Under each Goal is a set of Actions, which mainly apply to the work of the Organization, but also include encouraging and assisting members to take various steps at national level. These actions are to be prioritised by the ITTO as it develops its annual work programmes. The Goals relating to Economic Information and Market Intelligence speak of improving marketing, distribution and market access of exports from sustainably managed sources, although the actions do not seem to be related to the notion of sustainable management.

The ITTO has been criticised for not having the mechanisms for ensuring that there is some follow-through on these policy pronouncements at the national level.[11] Indeed, a similar criticism can be levelled at it in relation to its international policies, given the disappointing implementation of the original Year 2000 Objective and the slowness in operationalising the Bali Partnership Fund. But at the national level, for example, no country has yet enforced any of the ITTO guidelines, nor have these guidelines been used as a basis for the development of national level guidelines.[12] In addition, it has been acknowledged that despite several projects that assist countries in developing forest management plans, very few of these have been actually implemented.[13] This must be put into the context of the ITTO's mission as a "facilitator" and a forum for dialogue among members, but still there could be a more structured means for national reporting so as to evaluate compliance by members. Indeed, while the various policy documents contain many worthwhile statements, they tend to be at a level of generality that makes it difficult to assess how effective the implementation is on the ground.

Although the ITTO budget for projects is not enormous, it is also not negligible; at present it is still not certain how much the Bali Fund will add. However, the lack of clear feedback loops between field projects and policy development makes it difficult to judge the ITTO's actual impact. The ITTO has recently developed new terms of reference for the Expert Panel for the Technical Appraisal of ITTO Project and Pre-Project Proposals to ensure that such proposals are consistent with the Year 2000 Objective. Developing a better communications system is rightly a priority of the Organization.

At a more fundamental level, the ITTO would benefit from resolving the unspoken, but surely present, conflict in its objectives – and indeed the objectives of members – between enhancing revenues through trade promotion and encouraging conservation. Often these have been the subject of division among producer and consumer nations. But even some of the ITTO's own technical work has shed light on this inconsistency.[14] Indeed, the ITTA 1994 appears to tilt the balance in favour of free trade, in stipulating that "Nothing in the Agreement authorizes the use of measures to restrict or ban international trade in, and in particular as they concern imports of and utilization of, timber and timber products."[15] Other contradictions appear between pursuit of conservation and development objectives.[16]

---

[11] *See*, e.g. D. Cassells, *Considerations for Effective International Cooperation in Tropical Forest Conservation and Management*, unpublished (on file with the authors), 1994, at 14.

[12] D. Humphries, *Hegemonic ideology and the ITTO*, in J. Vogler and M. Imber (eds), The Environment & International Relations, at 224.

[13] S. Korsgaard, *Forest Management Planning in the ITTO Context*, Tropical Forest Update, vol.7, no.3, 1997.

[14] *See* D. Humphries, *supra* at note 12, at 226

[15] Article 36.

[16] *See* D. Humphries, *supra* at note 12, at 226.

The ITTO would need to become more proactive if it is to reassert its capacity to be a conceptual leader. Although it can be credited with some pioneering conceptual work in the late 1980s and early 1990s, more recently it seems more reactive or less willing to embrace new developments. For example, proposals for the ITTC to adopt resolutions which call for respecting the livelihoods of forest dwelling peoples consistently failed, although the ITTA 1994 calls for forest management activities "with due regard for the interests of local communities dependant on forest resources."[17]

Another example concerns certification and labelling of forest products. As early as 1989, proposals were made for the ITTO to encourage labelling to promote sustainably produced timber, however these were not adopted. More recently, the ITTO has engaged consultants to produce some useful analytic studies, but it is not apparent whether this will lead to eventual action.[18] There are clearly limitations to what the ITTO can achieve on this, since its mandate is limited to tropical timber trade, whereas issues relating to certification and labelling are global. Indeed, although it has responsibility over trade and environment issues in the IFF process, the ITTO contribution has tended to be rather technical and has not so far broken new ground.

Perhaps this partly reflects the ITTO's admirable, but perhaps unwieldy, tradition of operating by consensus.[19] One commentator has put it as follows:

> Consensual decision-making procedures, far from leading to agreement among the ITTO's membership, have served to mask disagreements… Tropical forest conservation, while central to the ITTO's mandate, has not been allowed to challenge the sovereignty of producer members over their forests, to interfere with free trade or to prevent the exploitation of tropical forests for timber products.[20]

2. Food and Agriculture Organization of the UN

The Food and Agriculture Organization of the UN (FAO) is a very significant international institution which deals with forests, in terms of its mandate, amount of activities, technical expertise, human resources, and reach into the national and regional levels. It is the Task Manager in the UN System for Chapter 11 of Agenda 21 and is the chair of the Inter-agency Task Force on Forests (ITFF). It is the key focal point under the IPF/IFF for national forest programmes, fragile ecosystems affected by desertification and drought, air-borne pollution, assessment of multiple benefits of forests, and criteria and indicators. These functions have led it to either convene or participate in numerous global and regional activities. In addition to the Committee on Forestry (COFO) – whose members are heads of forest services and other senior government officials who meet every two years – and the Regional Forestry Commissions, the FAO has 5 other statutory bodies dealing with various forest issues.[21]

---

[17] Article 1(j).

[18] *See* A. Bennett and A. Smith, *Directions and Directives – Whither ITTO*), Tropical Forest Update, vol. 7, no. 1, 1997.

[19] *See* Article 12 of ITTA 1983.

[20] *See*, D. Humphries, *supra* at note 12, at 227.

[21] The Committee on Mediterranean Forestry Questions, the International Poplar Commission, the Advisory Committee on Paper and Wood Products, the Advisory Committee on Forestry Education, and the Panel of Experts of Forest Gene Resources.

The FAO has had forestry on its agenda since its inception.[22] Its mission in forestry is:

> To enhance human well-being through the sustainable management of the world's trees and forests.[23]

Its goals are environmental, economic and social, while its implementation strategies include fulfilling its mandated role (a neutral forum that facilitates policy and technical dialogue, source of information, technical assistance, policy advice, investment advice and research support), setting priorities, and building partnership with others.[24]

Currently, the FAO forest programme employs 75 full-time professionals, plus approximately 250 contracted employees with a broad range of skills. Membership in the FAO is now up to 174 countries, with all major forested countries as members, with the significant exception of Russia, which has special liaison status.

The FAO's approach is meant to be comprehensive and interdisciplinary.[25] Its vast programme is divided into three themes: forest resources, forest products and forest policy and planning. The Programme on Forest Resources includes activities relating to the assessment and monitoring of forests (e.g. Global Forest Resource Assessment, which is published every 10 years), preparation and promotion of guidelines for management of forests and their biological diversity, and development of criteria and indicators for sustainable forest management, management of protected areas and implementing the Desertification Convention. The Programme on Forest Products promotes environmentally sound use of all types of forest products, as well as trade promotion and marketing. The Programme on Forest Policy and Planning deals with the policy, institutional and socio-economic aspects of forest development, including national forest pro-grammes, capacity-building, and community forestry. Included in the latter are activities in a variety of issues, such as communal management, conflict management, gender and participatory processes. The scope of activities is certainly very wide, perhaps understandably given the many demands on it, but the FAO has also been criticised by its members for failing to sufficiently prioritise.[26]

The FAO also has direct reach to the field level, through its Forestry Field Programme, which provides technical assistance to developing countries. Although it no longer finances all its own field projects, and instead is mainly an executing agency for bilateral and multilateral donors, this aspect of the FAO programme is still significant.[27] Nonetheless, the FAO's impact in the field may be limited by a decrease in presence in developing countries.[28]

---

[22] Article I(1) of the FAO Constitution provides that agriculture includes forestry and primary forestry products, while Article I(2)(c) gives the Organization the mandate to promote the conservation of natural resources.

[23] FAO, Secretariat Note, *FAO's Strategic Plan for Forestry*, European Forestry Commission, Twenty-Ninth Session, 19-23 October 1998.

[24] *Id.*

[25] Information in this paragraph comes from Secretariat Note, Committee on Forestry, Thirteenth Session, Medium-Term Strategy (1998-2003) and Priorities for the Programme of Work and Budget 1998-99, 1997 and FAO, *FAO, Forests and Forestry, available from FAO Web site* <http://www.fao.org/>.

[26] *See* FAO COFO, Report of the Thirteenth Session, 10-13 March 1997, p. 41

[27] The FAO also contributes about 16% of the finances needed for the field programme – the remaining comes from national trust funds and UNDP.

[28] M. Simula, *Effective Coordination Mechanisms in Financing Sustainable Forestry Develop-ment*, 1996.

While the breadth of the FAO's activities in forests is impressive, the amount of funding allocated to these activities is comparatively small. The most recent meeting of the COFO

> Expressed concern at the limited budgetary allocation for forestry in general and at the fact that the share of forestry in the overall FAO budget remained limited and therefore inconsistent with the post-UNCED importance of forestry in relation to sustainable forest management, desertification, climate change and the conservation of biological diversity. It is strongly recommended that the FAO allocate additional resources for this programme period.[29]

The FAO was the subject of considerable criticism for its role in the ill-fated Tropical Forestry Action Programme. These criticisms went to the heart of FAO's administration and resulted in loss of political and financial support for the TFAP. At the global level, the FAO's credibility was further challenged by its open support during UNCED for a new convention on forests, against the will of some developing countries. At the time of the IPF's establishment, it was considered significant that the CSD did not choose to have the IPF administered by the FAO. NGOs, especially, preferred shifting the global debate away from COFO, which was perceived to be dominated by industry interests. Even with the FAO, COFO was not perceived as living up to its full potential.[30]

However, in recent years, the FAO has made some significant changes. A key one has been to make the promotion of the national forest programme a priority.[31] Although the FAO is not the only international organization dealing with NFPs, the shift towards a bottom-up, country led approach meets some of the criticisms levelled at it in relation to the TFAP. FAO's approach is at both international and national levels.[32] At the former, the Organization's role includes promoting the concept, mobilising the interest of financial institutions, preparing operational and methodological guidelines, liaising with international partners and monitoring and evaluating the performance. At the national level, the FAO provides support to countries in the form of information and advice on the guiding principles, guidance for forest sector reviews, formulation of policies and legislation, support to national institutions with the aim of integrating the management of forest resources with sustainable socio-economic development and environmental protection.

The FAO has recently become more vocal on more macro-level issues, which may be giving it a greater role in raising forests to a higher position on the national agenda. The FAO has also become more transparent, in response to criticisms that it was not sufficiently open to NGOs, as compared to private industry, and now makes efforts to seek input from NGOs.[33] The Organization has also become more effective at transmitting information on its key areas – e.g. its internet site is very comprehensive.

The FAO's forest programme has been evolving and will likely continue to do so. Its diverse activities fill an important need and it remains the only permanent multilateral body that deals with forest issues. However, its record is not unblemished by controversy and failure. One of the reasons

---

[29] FAO COFO, Report of the 13th Session, 10-13 March 1997, Paragraph 40. Research on FAO financing must differentiate between core programme and additional project funds.

[30] D. Harcharik, *FAO forestry – responding to change*, 182 Unasylva, available from FAO web site.

[31] Perhaps also of significance is that these activities are coordinated by the Forest Programmes Coordination and Information Unit attached to the office of the Assistant Director-General of the Forestry Department.

[32] This information comes from the FAO web site, *supra* at note 25.

[33] *Id.*

why some NGOs, and even some governments, quietly, have opposed a new forest convention is because of a fear that a non-transparent, development-interest dominated FAO would be the institutional home for such an instrument. While this is changing for the better, and its experience as chair of the ITFF has been received mostly positively, some suspicion remains. This makes the consideration of IFF Category III issues even more complicated, while at the same time reinforcing the need to have the debate under this point based on a comprehensive and holistic evaluation of alternatives.

3. The World Bank

The World Bank (which includes the International Bank for Reconstruction and Development and the International Development Association) has the overarching goal of helping borrowing governments reduce poverty and increased economic growth. Strategies for achieving this goal include strengthening economies and expanding markets through financing of a range of projects and programmes in developing countries. The Bank's lending averaged US$22.3 billion per year during the fiscal years 1991-95.[34] As of fiscal year 1997, the Bank's total portfolio was reported to include 1,766 projects worth a total of $141 billion.[35]

The World Bank has committed a total of over US$1.8 billion in assistance for forest projects since last revising its forest policy in 1991,[36] and describes itself as "the largest lender to developing countries for forest conservation and management."[37] Equally important, many other World Bank loans significantly affect forests, including infrastructure loans for road or pipeline construction, agricultural loans, or structural adjustment loans. A prominent feature of Bank forest policy is a ban on financing the logging of natural forests.[38] The Bank also has free-standing projects on forests, watershed management and land-use.

In 1997 the Bank initiated a review of its forest policy. This study was intended to augment a 1994 study that had reviewed the analysis, content and design of forest-related projects, but had not evaluated impacts because it took place only three years after the adoption of the 1991 policy.[39]

---

[34] Peter Bosshard, Carlos Heredia, David Hunter & Francis Seymour, *Lending Credibility: New Mandates and Partnerships for the World Bank* 4 (Washington: WWF et al., 1996).

[35] Anne Bichsel & Korinna Horta, *Leapfrog into Mainstreaming and Jump-Start the Learning Process* 2 (Berne, Washington: Swiss Coalition of Development Organizations/Environment Defense Fund, 1998).

[36] This and other information about the IBRD is available through the World Bank web site's pages on forests and forestry via <http://WBLN0018.worldbank.org/ESSD/FORESTPOL-E.NSF/MAINVIEW>. The source for the loan figures: minutes of February 1998 meeting between Bank and NGOs, Washington, D.C., available at same web site.

[37] World Bank/WWF Forest Alliance Press Release: Protected Forest Area Triples in Brazil's Amazon: Decree Signed by Brazilian President, Washington, April 29, 1998, available on Web at <http://www-esd.worldbank.org/wwf/news.htm>.

[38] Some observers argue that the existing policy's natural forest logging ban has little practical impact on logging. Logging is so profitable in many countries that it continues steadily without Bank financing. However, many NGOs believe that the ban has important symbolic value in that it acknowledges that the logging of primary forests is contrary to the Bank's stated objective to alleviate poverty.

[39] *See* 1994 Review of Implementation of the Forest Sector Policy: Summary, document available on Web at <http://WBLN0018.worldbank.org/ESSD/FORESTPOL-E.NSF/MAINVIEW>.

Bank management noted that forests were in crisis world-wide and were "continuing to deteriorate at an alarming rate so time remains essential if the World Bank is to further assist in reducing the pressures on forests and strengthening the poverty reducing potential of forests."[40] Outstanding questions about the review include whether it will cover other sectors that significantly affect forests, and the breadth and depth of consultations with interested parties, including forest dwelling people in borrowing countries.

Another recent initiative is the alliance announced in 1997 between the Bank and the conservation NGO the World Wildlife Fund (WWF). The alliance is aimed at conserving 10 percent of the world's forests by 2000.[41] To achieve this goal, the Bank will assist its client countries with setting aside 50 million hectares of forests in new protected areas and bring 200 million hectares of forests in production under independent certification by 2005. According to the Bank, twenty-two countries have pledged to achieve the goal of placing at least 10 percent of their forest types in protected areas by the year 2000.[42]

The Bank has also organized a "CEO Forum" involving consultations with chief executive officers from the timber industry. The goal is to encourage them to reform policies and practices to move toward sustainable forest management. Finally, the new environmental ombudsman/ compliance adviser position now being established by the International Finance Corporation (IFC) and the Multilateral Investment Guarantee Agency (MIGA)[43] – two additional organizations within the World Bank Group – could also be relevant to forests to the extent that they are affected by IFC or MIGA-supported activities, in that communities affected by the impacts of those activities on forests will be able to raise concerns with this official.

As a general matter, the Bank has at its disposal tremendous human resources in terms of technical expertise. Further research would be useful on the nature of these resources in areas relevant to forests. This could be carried out, for instance, through interviews with responsible Bank officials as well as non-governmental observers.

The Bank efforts to mainstream global environmental objectives such as biodiversity are also relevant to forest conservation. So far, indications are that these efforts have not achieved success. A recent independent evaluation of the Global Environment Facility concluded that the GEF's implementing agencies, in particular the World Bank, had failed to "mainstream" the GEF's environmental objectives into their overall portfolios of activities.[44] Specifically, the evaluation concluded "that the Bank has failed to mainstream the global environment in its regular portfolio of projects in the biodiversity and climate focal areas, that it has not taken steps to create the staff incentives necessary to put global environmental concerns on a par with traditional bank business, [and] that it has not systematically integrated global environmental objectives into economic or sector work." However, the Bank has succeeded over the years in taking some steps to consider environmental impacts in its operations, and there are opportunities to seek further improvement.

---

[40] Minutes of July 1998 meeting with NGOs, available on Web (address cited above).

[41] World Bank/WWF Forest Alliance Press Release: Protected Forest Area Triples in Brazil's Amazon: Decree Signed by Brazilian President, Washington, April 29, 1998, available on Web at <http://www-esd.worldbank.org/wwf/news.htm>.

[42] *Id.* For instance, the Brazilian government announced in April 1998 a commitment to "establish 25 million hectares ... of new protected forest areas by the year 2000," billed as "the single largest forest conservation bid ever in the Amazon." *Id.*

[43] *See* IFC, Press Release No. 99/39, Washington, D.C., October 22, 1998. Available on IFC web site at <http://www.ifc.org/pressroom/Archive/1998/9939/9939.html>.

[44] *See* Overall Performance Study of the Global Environment Facility, Executive Summary, available on GEF web site, <http://www.gefweb.org/default.htm>.

Another aspect of the Bank relevant for forests though not specifically a forest programme is the independent inspection panel. Formed in 1993, the panel provides a channel through which local citizens whose environment is affected negatively by a Bank-funded project can bring a complaint that the project violates Bank policies and procedures. A number of cases have involved damage to forests. The panel provides a mechanism that can help improve or remedy design or implementation of specific projects. By allowing those affected by projects to petition for an open investigation by a neutral arbiter, the inspection panel brings both specific project defects and deeper policy problems to the attention of the highest levels of the Bank, enhancing opportunities for institutional reform.

Finally, it should be noted that the Bank is the lead agency for the ITFF work on "valuation of forest goods and services" and "economic instruments, tax policies and land tenure". Although an original member of the ITFF, the Bank was not a very visible actor during the IPF. Its contribution to the IFF remains to be seen.

Further research is needed on the forest-related programmes of the Bank, the Bank's relevant strengths and weaknesses, and prospects for future contributions to achievement of the Rio goals for forests. This research could draw upon interviews of Bank and governmental officials, non-governmental commentators and analysts, and members of affected communities. It could investigate more thoroughly specific points, such as the outcomes of the inspection panel's investigations into projects with forest impacts.

4. UN Development Programme

The UN Development Programme (UNDP) has a long history of involvement in forest issues, mainly in the provision of technical assistance. It was one of the original partners in the TFAP and now links forest problems in a more cross-sectoral fashion with its overall goal of poverty alleviation and sustainable human development. Forest issues are currently dealt with mainly by its Sustainable Energy and Environment Division.[45]

UNDP spends approximately $50 million/year on technical assistance to forest-related programmes in at least 70 countries. These activities are supported through core funding, and include traditional forest management activities, as well as watershed management and soil conservation projects that incorporate the forest sector. UNDP also runs the Forest Capacity Programme, which was established in 1993 to support the development of capacity in developing countries to formulate and implement national forest programmes. Present funding for the FCP is provided by UNDP and special funds pledged or contributed by the Governments of the Netherlands and Sweden in the amount of approximately US$3.3 million.[46] The Forest Capacity Programme, which works closely with UNDP's larger Capacity 21 programme, is now active in several countries.

UNDP is one of the implementing agencies of the Global Environment Facility. One result is that UNDP is now responsible for at least 80 projects in the biodiversity and climate change focal areas, many of which have forest elements, for approximately $250 million. Another is that UNDP managed the GEF Small Grants Programme, of which the vast majority of projects it funds relate to forests.

---

[45] Most of the information on UNDP comes from UNDP Sustainable Energy and Environment Division, *Programme on Forests*, 1998.

[46] UNDP, 1997 Annual Report for Capacity 21, available from UNDP web site <http://www.undp.org>.

UNDP was the lead agency for the IPF for the programme elements on "underlying causes of deforestation and forest degradation" and "international cooperation in financial assistance and technology transfer for sustainable forest management". In the latter capacity, it convened an intersessional workshop on "Financial Mechanisms and Sources of Finance for Sustainable Forestry". It has continued to be the focal point in the ITFF on financial issues.

Most recently, UNDP has developed a Programme on Forests for 1997-2000. This programme, which has a $3.55 million budget, has the following development objective:

> to promote sustainable forest management, and related public and private sector partnership, at the country level, in order to safeguard the contribution of forests to sustainable livelihoods and the sustainable development goals of countries.

It contains three components: identifying successful strategies for sustainable forest management, strengthening national forest programmes and forest partnership agreements as strategies to promote sustainable forest management, and developing innovative financing for sustainable forest management. This Programme constitutes UNDP's follow-up to the IPF Proposals for Action.

UNDP is clearly a critically important actor in the provision of much needed field level technical assistance. It has also found a useful niche for itself in the international policy process, by focusing on financial mechanisms for sustainable forest management. Indeed, the IPF discussions on this were enriched by inputs relating to new ideas, such as forest partnership agreements and other public/private partnerships. It remains to be seen whether UNDP's potential for developing feedback loops between field realities and global policy making will be fulfilled. Further research, which should include interviewing project managers as well as managers at UNDP headquarters, should focus in particular on this point.

5. UN Environment Programme

The UN Environment Programme has a relatively modest capacity to deal with forest issues. It was, and continues to be, the lead agency during the IPF for the programme element on "needs and requirements of countries with low forest cover" and it currently has the lead in the ITFF for "underlying causes of deforestation" and "forest conservation". It also has been collaborating with FAO in facilitating the development of regional criteria and indicators for Dry-Zone Africa and the Near East. In 1998, UNEP became involved with other UN entities in preparing emergency action plans aimed at tackling the environmental consequences of forest fires in Indonesia and Amazonia.

UNEP's forest work falls under its programme on "Caring for Biological Resources", which potentially allows it to create some useful synergies with other biodiversity related UNEP activities. While many of the elements of the UNEP Programme of Work on this theme are relevant to forests, the draft Programme of Work for 2000-2001 indicates a plan to continue playing a largely technical and facilitating role on forest issues.

UNEP's contribution to the international forest regime must be assessed in light of its limited financial resources and its catalytic approach. By focusing on regions such as dry-zone Africa and the Near East, UNEP has filled a necessary niche. More broadly, UNEP can be an important voice for conservation within the ITFF, given that many of the other members are concerned with other aspects of forests. Its responsibility for "underlying causes" is daunting, given the enormity of the topic, and it cannot be expected that UNEP action alone will be sufficient. But given the proper funds and other support from partners, UNEP can make an important technical, if not policy, contribution in dealing with this crucial topic.

Further research on UNEP should examine the new Programme of Work which will be approved in February 1999 by the UNEP Governing Council and evaluate the success of its inter-sessional work on "underlying causes".

6. Global Environment Facility [47]

The Global Environment Facility (GEF) provides grants and concessional funding to eligible developing countries and countries with economies in transition for projects and programmes that protect the global environment and promote sustainable economic growth. GEF projects and programmes are managed through three implementing agencies: the UN Development Programme (UNDP), the UN Environment Programme (UNEP) and the World Bank. The GEF Secretariat is defined as functionally independent from the three implementing agencies. It reports to and services the Council and Assembly of the GEF.

Originally set up as a pilot programme in 1991, the GEF was restructured and replenished with over US $2 billion in 1994, to cover the "agreed incremental costs" of activities that benefit the global environment in four focal areas: climate change; biological diversity; international waters; and stratospheric ozone. Activities concerning land degradation, primarily desertification and deforestation, as they relate to the four focal areas, are also eligible for funding. Both the Framework Convention on Climate Change and the Convention on Biological Diversity have designated the GEF as their funding mechanism on an interim basis.

The GEF is striving for universal participation and currently 156 countries are participants. Countries may be eligible for GEF funds in one of two ways: (1) if they are eligible for financial assistance through the financial mechanism of either the Climate Change Convention or the Convention on Biological Diversity; or (2) if they are eligible to borrow from the World Bank (IBRD and/or IDA) or receive technical assistance grants from UNDP through a Country Programme. A country must be a party to the Climate Change Convention or the Convention of Biological Diversity to receive funds from the GEF in the relevant focal area. GEF policies state that projects must be country driven, incorporate consultation with local communities and, where appropriate, involve non-governmental organizations in project implementation.

Within the biodiversity focal area, the GEF has adopted an "operational programme" concerning forest ecosystems. Consistent with decisions of the CBD COP, it emphasises an "ecosystem approach." Its objectives are to conserve biological resources in forest ecosystems through (1) systems of conservation areas emphasising areas at risk, and (2) "sustainable use forest management" that "combines production, socio-economic and biodiversity goals," erecting use management regimes that range from strict protection within reserves to full scale use in other areas. The programme envisions a wide range of conservation and sustainable development activities eligible for funding.

More research is needed on the forest-related activities of the GEF and its strengths and weaknesses in relation to forests. This could involve contacts with responsible GEF Secretariat officials as well as responsible officials in the implementing agencies and non-governmental observers. In the meantime, some of the general findings about GEF activities of the recent independent evaluation of the GEF may have implications for the GEF's forest related activities. The evaluation noted that the GEF's resources are "small in comparison with funding needs in the focal areas," including biodiversity. Yet the GEF seemed to have been successful in leveraging significant amounts of cofinancing, including small but growing amounts of private sector financing.

---

[47] The first three paragraphs of this section are adapted from material on the GEF web site, available at <http://www.gefweb.org/intro/gefintro.htm>.

Perhaps the most important finding of the independent evaluation was that the GEF had failed to facilitate the mainstreaming of biodiversity or other global environmental concerns into the World Bank's programmes and policies, as discussed in Part V.A above.[48] The importance of this goal is illustrated by a comparison of the Bank's outstanding portfolio of $141 billion in 1,766 projects to the GEF's portfolio, which includes $1.6 billion in 230 projects.[49]

7. International Monetary Fund ("IMF")

The IMF's mission is to promote international monetary cooperation, to facilitate growth in international trade, to promote exchange stability, and to make financial resources available to members having temporary difficulties with balance of payments.[50] Established in 1945 at the Bretton Woods conference, the IMF has 182 members and is headquartered in Washington. In early 1998 the IMF had financial arrangements for about US $37 billion with 58 countries.

IMF loans and credits are typically conditioned on the borrower government's adoption of policies of adjustment and reform intended to restore and maintain economic stability. The IMF also monitors and reports on members' exchange policies and provides technical assistance to members regarding fiscal and monetary policy.

IMF activities can have indirect but potentially damaging impacts on forests. For instance, as a condition for receiving assistance, the IMF may require reduction of government budgets, damaging social safety nets and poverty relief programmes that help prevent the very poor from using forests unsustainably.

IMF conditions may also require expansion of exports, which leads to expanded commodity crop production or timber harvesting, leading to loss or degradation of forests. For instance, in Indonesia, the IMF has pushed the government to increase palm oil exports and encourage greater foreign investments in palm oil plantations.[51] Yet the burning of forests to make way for expansion of oil palm plantations has been identified as the leading cause of the massive forest fires in 1997 and 1998. Companies operating in East Kalimantan are also reported to have seized forest lands of indigenous peoples for conversion to oil palm plantations.[52]

It was not possible to research fully the linkages between the IMF's programmes and forests, or its strengths and weaknesses with respect to forests, for this report. Further research could be useful, especially research aimed at identifying the specific ways in which IMF assistance conditions affect forests, and options for policies that would encourage economic recovery in developing countries that sustains and does not threaten forests. This research would draw upon interviews of IMF and governmental officials, non-governmental commentators and analysts, and members of affected communities, to the extent that impacts can be ascertained. Economic analysis could be a useful component of such research.

---

[48] *See* Rob Edwards & Sanjay Kumar, *Dust to Dust*, NEW SCIENTIST, 6 June 1998, at 18.

[49] *See* Bichsel & Horta, *supra* n. 83, at 2.

[50] This paragraph is adapted from *The IMF at a Glance* (1998), published on IMF web site <http://www.imf.org/>.

[51] *See* Accounting for the Environment with the National Wildlife Federation, *Delay in Accounting Reforms at International Monetary Fund Fuels Forest Fires, Perpetuates Poverty* (Washington: Accounting for the Environment, 1998).

[52] *See* Accounting for the Environment, *supra* n. 97.

8. Inter-agency Task Force on Forests

The Inter-agency Task Force on Forests (ITFF) was created during the IPF as an informal high level entity. Most of the organizations surveyed in this chapter are members of the ITFF.[53] Its objective is

> to secure and coordinate support from its members for the IPF/IFF process in a manner which builds on the agencies' respective strengths, minimizes duplication and overlaps, makes the most efficient use of existing resources, and fosters partnership and collaboration, but also assists many countries in national level implementation of the IPF proposals for action.[54]

Following the conclusion of the IPF in 1997, the ITFF developed the "Inter-agency Partnership on Forests: Implementation of the IPF Proposals for Action by the ITFF". This document was the basis for discussions among the ITFF members about their respective work programmes and potential modalities for collaborating with other partners. Its focus on implementation issues is significant. An update is currently being prepared.

The ITFF has been considered a useful mechanism, within its limits. There had been some concerns raised at the beginning of its operation about its transparency, but more recent efforts to publicise its work and engage NGOs is to be welcomed. The ITFF may eventually form the basis for a more permanent mechanism for coordinating the activities of international institutions, but this would require a clearer and more definite mandate and a broader membership to encompass the other relevant actors in the international forest regime. Ultimately, though, better coordination will depend on the extent to which there are clear messages on substance from the international forest policy process.

III. Preliminary Conclusions

This survey has revealed that while there is considerable activity undertaken by international institutions in relation to forests, there is room for improvement. As the IFF noted at its second session, "there is significant unrealized potential for further strengthening and mobilizing the capacity of existing international and regional organizations ..."[55] As it further notes, what is needed is increased work on fostering synergies and clarifying respective roles and work in relation to UNCED follow-up.[56]

It is expected that the IFF Secretariat will prepare in-depth analyses which will examine issues such as the degree and effectiveness of international cooperation on forest-related work. This analysis will greatly benefit from an evaluation of the work of existing international institutions, which is based on their mandates, capacity, and impacts at the global policy levels and in the field.

---

[53] The ITFF's members are: Centre for International Forestry Research (CIFOR), FAO, ITTO, Secretariat of the CBD, UN Department for Policy Coordination and Sustainable Development, UNEP, UNDP and the World Bank.

[54] *Supra*, note 1.

[55] IFF Secretariat, Report of the Second Session of the Intergovernmental Forum on Forests, 24 August – 4 September 1998, unofficial version/advance unedited text.

[56] *Id.*

Regional Legal Arrangements for Forests: the Case of Central America

By Grethel Aguilar and Marco González

I. Introduction

This paper will analyse the regional legal and policy framework for forests in Central America. Beginning in the 1980s, the region has developed various instruments aimed at enhancing cooperation relating to forests, including the Central American Forest Convention, which was the world's first regional treaty on forests. These are examined here as a case study.

After surveying the state of forest resources in Central America, including an identification of the main causes of deforestation, the paper will analyse the region's policy and legal instruments relating to forests. The Central American Forest Convention will be particularly highlighted. Finally, the reasons for the success of that Convention will be identified. The Annex describes the evolution of national legislation on forests in the region.

II. The State of Forest Resources in Central America

The potential for forestry in Central America is considerable, with approximately 19 million hectares of forested areas and 13 million hectares of land with a forestry potential that is currently being used for other purposes. This latter amount represents approximately 64% of the region's territory. However, an estimated 400,000 hectares of forests are lost annually. The recent El Niño phenomenon, which led to massive forest fires, has generated a further loss of 1.5 million hectares of forests, and economic losses estimated in the order of US $1 billion 1998.[1]

The greatest levels of deforestation in Central America occur in low-lying lands covered with tropical rainforests. It is estimated that two-thirds of this forest loss have occurred within the past three decades. This deforestation has, in turn, led to accelerated deterioration of watersheds, high erosion rates and loss of biodiversity.

The causes of the deforestation are diverse. The two fundamental ones are: changes in land use in forested areas (especially agricultural conversion) and the massive use of firewood for energy needs. For example, regarding the latter cause, in Belize 33%, and in Guatemala 85%, of homes use firewood for domestic purposes.[2] Indeed, only 20% of the total production of processed timber goes to the international market. Poverty is a major driving force that underlies these causes. Other important factors include accelerated population growth (at an average rate of 2.8% per annum, which means that it doubles every 25 years), increased unemployment in productive sectors, and credit and land titling policies, as well as subsidies, that favour extensive cattle ranching.[3] This suggests that policies to address deforestation should focus less on forests, *per se*, and more on wider development issues that are related to macro-economic policies and other sectoral agendas, especially those relating to agrarian and land-tenure policies.

Although the area under coniferous forests has not diminished at the same rate as the broadleaf forests, these areas too are suffering from significant genetic degradation and a progressive reduction in the volume of timber stands. The degradation of coniferous forests is critical to the timber industry and for the energy supply in rural areas in Honduras and Guatemala. These two countries alone provide 90% and 60% of the region's saw-wood and, as alluded to above, their

---

[1] El Periodico, Guatemala June 25,1998.

[2] Rodríguez Jorge y otros, *Estado del Ambiente y los Recursos Naturales en Centroamérica San José Costa Rica*, Union Mundial para la Naturaleza, CCAD, 1998.

[3] Informe 1991. Plan de Accion Forestal para Centro America (PAFCA). 1991

populations depend to a high degree, up to 60%, on these timber sources for their energy consumption.

These factors are exacerbated by problems within the forestry industry itself, which prevent it from using all available forest resources in an optimal manner. In fact, only a limited number of species are commercially exploited by the industry (practically geared around two major species of hardwoods: Mahogany – *Sweetenia macrophylla* – and Cedar- *Cedrela Odoratta*). This reliance on just two species is due to an obsolete industrial base geared to primary transformation, and the lack of qualified personnel in forestry sciences.

Objectively, therefore, it cannot be argued that the region has succeeded in curbing deforestation or in dealing with its social and economic causes. Nonetheless, as will be seen below, some achievements can be identified within the frameworks of the region's policy and legal instruments.

III. The Regional Framework

1. The Central American Convention on Environment

The Central American Convention on Environment, which created the Central American Commission on Environment and Development (CCAD), requires the CCAD to develop and harmonise environmental legislation and to "create a regional regime for environmental cooperation". The reason for this mandate was due, in part, to the concern expressed by the Presidents of Central America and the Prime Minister of Belize over the high levels of forest cover loss in the region and the increasing deterioration of the primary and secondary forests.

The Convention's general objective is the establishment of a regional regime for environmental cooperation to promote the optimal and rational use of natural resources in the region.[4] It then defines priority actions, *inter alia*: the protection of watersheds, the management of tropical forests and the valuation and protection of the region's natural heritage.

In order to attain these general and specific objectives, the Convention requires the establishment of cooperative linkages between countries of the region to attain sustainable development styles and to promote actions for the optimal and rational use of natural resources, the control of pollution and the maintenance of the ecological equilibrium.

To ensure the concretion of the regional regime for environmental cooperation, the Convention requires Parties to promote an environmental agenda that is participatory, democratic and decentralised. This requirement is far from easy to implement, since the constitution and environmental legislation of practically all of the countries of the region still insist in the legal fiction that natural resources are either national heritage or state property.[5]

2. The Central American Forest Action Plan

The CCAD's first task was to prepare the participatory processes called for by the Tropical Forest Action Plan for Central America (PAF-CA). The PAF-CA sought to evolve into a regional strategy

---

[4]   Article 1.

[5]   E.g. Article 102 Constitution of Nicaragua, Art 102, Art. 62 Law of the Environment of Panama, which declares that natural resources are in the public domain in the public interest.

which, following a prior assessment phase, would lead to the adoption of a viable action plan for the conservation of forests and their integration into a sustainable economy. Participation of local populations was meant to be a key element in this process. The original initiative of the PAF-CA originated among the national directors of the public agencies in charge of administrating forest resources.

The Plan was initially oriented by an assessment phase which identified the major problems facing the forestry sector in the region. An unavoidable conclusion of this assessment phase was that the potential of forest resources in Central America to provide goods and services was not being accorded its true value, and that those resources which were exploited were not being managed in a rational and sustainable fashion.[6]

The PAF-CA was approved by the presidents of Central America. Rather than being a regional strategy, however, it was more a portfolio of projects aimed at obtaining funding from international agencies without the presence of any real national counterparts in both institutional and financial terms.

The strategy did not attract sufficient support from the state apparatus in each of the region's countries. It tended to be co-opted into the agendas of the national offices of the Plan, which themselves had limited capacity to impact on national policies in a significant and real fashion. In some cases these offices began to compete with national forestry authorities. An illustration of this lack of effectiveness is that between 1990 and 1995 – i.e. prior to the launch of the PAF-CA and five years later – the region lost 2.5 million hectares of forest cover.[7]

3. The Central American Environmental Agenda

As part of the preparations for the United Nations Conference on Environment and Development (UNCED), the region's Heads of State decided that a situational assessment be prepared in relation to environmental management. This assessment concluded that traditional development models had resulted in inadequate management and degradation of the region's natural resource base, including forests. Among the priority actions recommended was the preparation and development of protection and conservation programmes for natural resources. This led the CCAD to prepare the Central American Environmental Agenda, which attempts to provide a framework for environmental management at a regional level.

4. The Sustainable Development Alliance (ALIDES)

In 1994, the Alliance for Sustainable Development (ALIDES) was established. ALIDES is a set of principles, policies and political procedures intended to enable a new development from a sustainable perspective. ALIDES is an innovative instrument, being a legally binding treaty framework for the regional integration process, in which the decisions and resolutions of presidential summits are legally binding. The objectives and environmental provisions stipulated in the Alliance, together with the Central America Environmental Agenda, constitute the frame-work for the national policies aimed at the sustainable management of forests.

---

[6]   PAF-CA, 1991, p.4

[7]   CCAD-State of the Environment and Natural Resources in Central America, 1998, p. 93

5. The Central American Forest Convention

Several other important instruments (both political and legal) were approved at a regional level to complement the PAF-CA. Of these, the most important and far-reaching is the 1993 Regional Convention for the Management and Conservation of Natural Forest Ecosystems and the Development of Forest Plantations ("Central American Forest Convention").

The Convention's main objectives are to:

- promote national and regional mechanisms to prevent changes in land use in areas under forest cover with forestry potential;
- rehabilitate deforested areas;
- reorient settlement policies on forest lands;
- create disincentives for actions which produce forest destruction;
- promote a process of land use planning with sustainable options.

The Central American Forest Convention not only deals with forest loss but strives to go further by enabling a regional policy that creates new policy options relating to land tenure and land use in areas earmarked for forestry and protection. It seeks to shift away from a system predominantly agrarian in focus (where the right to land is only granted to those persons who make "productive" use of it, which in many cases implies the destruction of forested lands), to one which promotes the conservation and sustainable use of forests. However, the Convention stops short of dealing with the region's poverty, which, as noted above, is a significant underlying cause of deforestation.

The Convention creates the Central American Council on Forests (CCAB), which is an essential and catalytic institution for promoting and coordinating different sectors and stakeholders in relation to forests. The CCAB reports directly to the CCAD, and involves all national agencies in charge of natural resources and the environment. The CCAB's members are the Directors of the Forest Services of the region's seven countries, as well as authorities designated by the governments of the region.

The CCAB, in conjunction with CCAD, is responsible for conducting the follow-up to and monitoring of the Forest Convention. It is primarily a technical body, which has been the driving force behind the formulation of a regional forestry policy. This has not been conducted in a fashion that is isolated from other components of the environmental agenda. On the basis of technical and policy criteria, it was decided that the Central American Council for Protected Areas (CCAP), created by the Central American Convention on Biodiversity, and the CCAB, would collaborate closely. The result is that the development of forest policies is conducted in parallel to the development of policies regarding protected areas, which include non-timber forest products and the environmental services derived from forest stands.

The CCAB also works towards harmonising forestry legislation in the region, by promoting instruments such as management plans, which are currently being incorporated into every piece of national legislation involving forests and the environment. CCAB has also been closely involved with efforts to define criteria and indicators for forest certification at a regional level (there are currently 70,000 hectares of certified forests under sustainable management in the region), which provides a regional model for granting forest management concessions. A regional strategy is also underway to prevent and mitigate forest fires and to create a regional market for certificates of carbon sequestration in the context of the UN Framework Convention on Climate Change and the Regional Convention on Climate Change.

In the following paragraphs, we present, in the order in which they appear in the Convention, the Convention's obligations, coupled with a report on their implementation:

1. *Parties shall consolidate a National and Regional System for Protected Wildlife Areas.*[8] This is a shared mandate with the Regional Convention on Biodiversity. Currently there has been progress obtained in the constitution of the Mesoamerican Biological Corridor, and the creation and strengthening of protected areas in border regions such as the Río San Juan, the Gulf of Honduras and of Fonseca.

2. *Parties shall develop appropriate programmes of agricultural and livestock development which take account of the productive value of forests, forest management, and reforestation for energy needs*[9] We have already mentioned reforestation plans and incentives, with their varying degrees of success. The plantations destined for firewood appear, however, to be the "Achilles Heel" of the reforestation programmes, since they have only been developed by large agro-industrial enterprises, such as sugar mills.

3. *Parties shall maintain a dynamic inventory, at a large scale, of their forest cover.*[10] This has been largely accomplished through regional cooperation in the use of geographic information systems.

4. *Parties shall create specific national funds to support financially national priorities.*[11] Currently there are Forest Funds in Costa Rica, Guatemala and Nicaragua (Environmental Fund) and the creation of such a fund is included in the proposed Forestry Law of El Salvador.

5. *Parties shall create mechanisms to guarantee the reinvestment of income generated from forests and secure credit for local groups who can develop forestry programmes.*[12] The forest laws of Guatemala and Costa Rica contemplate such arrangements and these mechanisms are beginning to function. This is indirectly complemented by national environmental funds – both private and public – which include among their eligible projects, reforestation and natural forest management projects in every country of the region.

6. *Parties shall strengthen regional processes for channel financial resources.*[13] The Central American Environmental Fund was constituted, and is now operational, having received funding from the GEF in the amount of US$15 million. CCAD has also received funds from the United States to forge a strategy for donors in the region.

7. *Parties shall modify their national accounting systems to allow for the introduction of environmental parameters.*[14] The environmental laws of Panama, Nicaragua, El Salvador and Honduras now have mandates to incorporate forestry resources in their national accounts.

---

[8]   Article 3.

[9]   Articles 3(b) (c).

[10] Article 3(e).

[11] Article 4(a).

[12] Article 4(b) (c).

[13] Article 4(d).

[14] Article 4(e).

8. *Parties shall establish mechanisms to control the illegal trade of flora, fauna, timber and other forest products.*[15] The 1995 Central American Treaty for Democratic Security requires governments, through their public security forces, to fight against the illegal trade in timber, and in species of fauna and flora".[16] One result has been the establishment of a regional coordination unit of CITES authorities, which helped create a common position for the 1997 CITES COP. This common position was especially important given that the listing of Mahogany was in issue at that meeting – the common position was to support the inclusion of this tree species on Appendix II.

9. *Parties shall promote public participation and shall recognise the rights of indigenous peoples and other inhabitants of forested areas.*[17] All countries in the region, with the exception of Nicaragua, have ratified the ILO Convention 169 on Indigenous Peoples. The Central American Council on Forests includes representatives of all stakeholders in civil society (indigenous peoples, producers, industry, and environmentalists) in its periodic working sessions, according to regulations approved in May 1997 in Managua, Nicaragua. Regional movements and institutions dedicated to community and indigenous agroforestry have thus emerged, and the CCAB has strengthened small-holder agriculturist organisations, by allowing them to be represented in the Central American Integration System through its Consultative Council. This forum has facilitated the replication of processes for community-base management of natural resources and small-scale forest management, as well as for training and exchanging appropriate technology.

10. *Parties shall strengthen their institutions, adopt National Forest Action Plans, creating environmental prosecutors offices, conducting studies and training related to forest management.*[18] All such Plans have been formally adopted. Currently, with the approval of the Law of the Environment in Panama, environmental prosecutors offices have been created in every country. Prosecutors have been trained in law enforcement through materials produced by the CCAD in close collaboration with NGOs involved in environmental law. At this point, in all countries, without exception, cases of forest infractions and felonies are being dealt with by the law courts.

11. The CCAD, in conjunction with the National Administrations for Environment and Development, shall create a Central American Council on Forests.[19] As mentioned, the Council was created in June 1993 in Panama City. It has an Executive Secretariat, and has promoted and approved regional policies on criteria and indicators, procedures, forest concessions, certification systems and forest laws.

As can be seen, the implementation of the Convention has so far been satisfactory, although not perfect. However, this is to be understood as only the beginning of a process that attempts to change a development model based on inappropriate uses of the land and unsustainable techniques. To transform a Central America run by agriculturists and cattle ranchers into a region combing agriculture and livestock with agro-forestry and forestry will take time.

But, the first results can already be seen. Nicaragua has recently undertaken a profound reform of its state apparatus, by which the Ministry of Agriculture and Livestock was transformed into the

---

[15] Article 4(f).

[16] Article 25(a).

[17] Article 5.

[18] Article 6.

[19] Article 7.

Ministry of Agriculture, Livestock and Forestry.[20] Similar processes are underway in other countries.

There is still much to be done, especially to incorporate environmental and sustainable use issues into the regional commercial agenda. This process began in July 1997 in Panama City, with a first meeting between the Ministers of Commerce and of Environment, at which a regional agenda was approved on trade and environment. This includes topics promoted by the forestry sector such as "green certificates" and the sale of environmental services of forests.

One must also take in account that although this convention regulates the management and conservation of forests in the region, there are factors which are not dealt with, such as the commercialisation of new forest species, international cooperation in relation to environmental services, and, as mentioned above, poverty. Furthermore, although Central America has been strengthened as a region, through the implementation of this Convention, to a large degree the results derived from this instrument will have to be measured in relation to the impact that external policies have on the forests of Central America.

6. Common Themes in Regional Environmental Treaties Relating to Forests

In addition to the Central American Forest Convention, both the Convention for the Conservation of Biodiversity and the Protection of Priority Protected Areas in Central America and the Central American Convention on Climate Change contain provisions relating to forests. Below is a set of relevant themes common to all three treaties:

1. *a regional position towards a common responsibility but differentiated between developed and developing countries concerning environmental degradation and the depletion of natural resources.* This means that industrialised countries must support the obligations assumed by developing countries in their efforts to conserve forests, through concrete actions and technological transfer based on the real needs of countries with tropical forests.

2. *a common position on the use of certain policy instruments such as environmental impact assessments, fiscal incentives and market mechanisms linked to forest management, and legal measures relating to the governance, control or prohibition on the use of forest resources.* Particularly relevant instruments are land use plans and forest management guidelines.

3. *recognition of the State's sovereign right to employ its natural resources, and, in particular, its forests.* This implies the freedom to apply its own policies and forest legislation, limited only by its international legal obligations.

4. *regional regime for environmental management.* This has enabled the development of a forest policy as part of broader environmental policy framework, which involves state agencies dealing with the environment and civil society.

5. *recognition of the obligation to refrain from national actions with transboundary impacts, as well as the obligation to inform about them when they occur.* To implement this, technical regulations have been established by the Regional Technical Commissions for

---

[20] Law for the Organization, Competences and Procedures of the Executive Power, 6 June 1998.

Environmental Auditing (CTAA) and the Technical Commission on Environmental Impact Assessment (CTEIA), both of which are created by the CCAD.

6. *increasing use of forest certification as a means to guarantee the sustainability of forest ventures.* Legal frameworks for certification are now being established to allow for the licensing of certifiers, as well as national licensing systems which aim at the development of standardised indicators, parameters, measures and procedures for forest certification. This will enable foreign and national investors in the forest sector to provide longer-term investments which aim at sustainable management, rather than ones based on short-term exploitation. This type of investment is now possible because of greater juridical security, transparency and public acceptance. It is important to stress that the principles, criteria and indicators now being developed at a national and regional level still need to incorporate criteria which reflect both biodiversity and social concerns in order to be most effective.

While there are other themes relating to forests which are not common to all three regional environmental treaties, there is some coherence established in implementation resulting from the fact that the CCAD is responsible for monitoring the implementation of each.

IV. Final Considerations

In order to understand why the implementation of the Central American Forest Convention has had some success, one must appreciate that this instrument is part of a wider process of regionalization, especially as regards the environment.

The second factor is the very wide participation and incorporation of the civil society views in this process in general, and in the sustainable management of forests in particular. The main institution for regional integration, the Central America Integration System (SICA) has an advisory body known as the Civil Society Consultative Council for Regional Integration, which includes many regional organisations directly involved in forestry issues. The same procedure has occurred in relation to the CCAD. Thus, from an early stage, civil society forestry and environmental groups have actively participated in the CCAD.

The third factor contributing to the region's modest success in forest issues is that the various instruments described in this paper have all been designed to function in a complementary and mutually supportive manner. For example, ALIDES and the Central American Environmental Agenda are considered key instruments that facilitate the implementation of the Central American Forest Convention. Of particular significance is, as noted above, that the Central American Forest Convention has been linked, through the CCAB, to the Central American Council on Protected Areas (CCAP), thus creating synergy in relation to sustainable management of forest protected areas. In fact, the Executive Secretary of the CCAB acts as Executive Secretary of CCAP. These two bodies are permanent fora for senior forestry and protected areas officers to meet, providing an opportunity for interacting, networking and cooperating to find creative responses and solutions. In addition, inputs from national professional associations of forest technicians and engineers has been important; in fact, the CCAB has promoted the foundation of such associations where they did not exist before.

The work of the CCAB has been further legitimated though a set of initiatives aimed at opinion building: i.e. publications (e.g. the Forestry Review), technical studies, and proposals for instruments (e.g. the Model Forest Law, the Indicators for Forestry Certification, the Model Rules for Forest Concessions). These initiatives have enjoyed widespread acceptance in the regional forestry sector.

Fourthly, the constant support within the CCAD for dealing with issues related to sustainable forestry management as a high priority has been significant. Since this is the highest regional political forum for environmental integration, the fact that the forestry issues and problems are consistently made part of CCAD Agenda have proven to be the way to reach the Presidents and highest decision-makers.

The final fact, which is certainly not the least important, has been the support received from many international agencies and NGOs, e.g. FAO, USAID, WWF, IUCN, FINNIDA, and SIDA. These bodies, through their regional offices, have provided financial resources and technical support, information and training to the CCAD, CCAB, and CCAP.

This paper has demonstrated that Central America now has valuable instruments for forest policy. These, combined with the fact that over the past ten years every country in the region has made significant progress in developing and implementing forest laws (see the Annex, below), has created a new vision of how to manage forest resources.

As a result, the conservation and rational management of the forest ecosystems constitute today a high priority in the regional political agenda. A key lesson to be drawn is that the regional instruments have been useful in leveraging change on the ground. That said, there are still many shortcomings and legal voids arising out of various pieces of national, regional and international law. This situation should improve over time, especially with continued external technical and financial support.

Annex

The Evolution of National Legislation on Forests in Central America

1. General Legislation

The roots of environmental legislation in Central America can be traced to the national Constitutions drafted towards the end of the 1970s. These laws were influenced by the principles set forth by the 1972 United Nations Conference on the Human Environment in Stockholm, as well as by the political events of the time, including the need to fight poverty and improve the quality of life of the region's inhabitants.

Terms such as "healthy environment" and "rational use of natural resources" are frequently found in these constitutions. This can be seen as a considerable achievement, especially since it integrates environment, as a matter of collective interest, into the policy framework of every government in the region.

Some constitutional norms expressly refer to forest resources. In Panama, Honduras and Nicaragua, the constitutions guarantee the sustainable use of natural resources and declare reforestation a collective interest, although in the case of Nicaragua reforestation is declared a national emergency.

In addition to constitutions, it is important to consider the regulations relating to forests which derive from general environmental laws. Environmental laws are the legal instruments that implement the constitutional mandates concerning the environment and reflect the principles of sustainable or rational use of natural resources, including forests. They establish the institutional structures and arrangements for the public regulation of these resources. Currently, all Central American countries have general environmental laws which, to a great extent, define national policies with regards to forest resources, as components of the environment, focusing principally on their conservation and rational use.

Two events are key in understanding the development of general environmental legislation in the region. In 1993, a project for a framework law for the environment and natural resources was approved in Mexico. That same year, the Central American Parliament (PARLACEN) revised this draft law and approved a model "Environmental Protection Law for the Sustainable Development of Central America". Both of these models have provided the basis upon which proposed laws have been drafted throughout the region. Since then, environmental laws have consistently defined clear forest policies and established the functions of environmental authorities so as to apply these policies from a sustainable perspective. In fact, in the majority of cases the development of environmental laws and new forest laws have occurred in parallel and inter-related processes.

2.   Specific Forest Legislation

New forest laws were ratified in 1993 in Panama, in 1996 in Costa Rica, and in Guatemala in 1997. In Belize, the forest law dates back to colonial times, although some modification was made following the 1980 Revision of Laws and Regulations. In Nicaragua, forest management is regulated by various pieces of legislation, including the 1967 Law for the Conservation, Protection and Development of the Country's Forest Wealth and the Emergency Law on the Rational Management of Forests of 1976, both which were amended and implemented through the 1993 Forestry Regulations.

The Forest Law of El Salvador was drafted in 1972, but has never had any implementing regulations enacted. In Honduras, the Forest Law[21] was reformed by the Law for the Modernisation of the Agricultural Sector.[22]

There are now proposals for forest laws pending in Nicaragua and in El Salvador, since both countries still have forest laws and regulations dating back to the 1970s. These law projects seek to establish systems based on positive incentives. In Nicaragua, the Forest Law Project No. 2, drafted in 1993 by IRENA (Institute for Natural Resources), has so far undergone five revisions. It was finally revised and amended on 15 December 1997, when the Commission for the Environment, along with other interested stakeholders, adopted a consensus motion, which was presented in a plenary session to the Legislative Assembly.

In Guatemala, notwithstanding that the current forest law still relies mainly on command and control instruments, a qualitative leap was made by also including fiscal and economic incentives for sustainable forest management in programmes geared at afforestation, reforestation, rural development and support to the forest industry.

In Costa Rica, a resolution from May 1997 assigns monetary value to the goods and services provided by forests as carbon sinks and producers of oxygen. In March, 1998, Panama recently adopted regulations to the 1993 Forest Law which operationalises, through specific instruments, the requirements of the Law of Incentives for Reforestation. These regulations also provide a clearer definition of the roles and relationships as between the Ministry of Finance and the Institute for Renewable Natural Resources (INRENARE). In addition, Panama also has a Law for Forestry Incentives dating from 1992.

---

[21]   Decree No. 885, 18.11.71 and related regulations of April, 1984.

[22]   Legislative Decree 31-92, of 06.05.92.

3.   Evaluation

As can be noted, legislation relating to forests in Central America has evolved considerably in the 1990s. The majority of countries are now endowed with new legislation, or at least new regulations to existing laws. This situation signals a clear shift in forest-related policies, placing more reliance on incentives and funds for conservation and management of forests. However, these laws, although paved with good intentions, are not sufficient in themselves to attain the sustainable management and conservation of the region's forests.

But the shift from being instruments that impose mainly sanctions and penalties for illegal activities, to ones which promote positive incentives and payment for environmental services is significant. This better responds to the needs of the population, the majority of which need forest resources for their subsistence and, in some cases, have faced obstacles in maintaining their livelihood from the existence of protected areas. Among their measurable effects is the fact that an estimated 35,000 hectares are reforested annually, amounting to a total of 416,126 hectares by 1998. This amount is equivalent to a reforestation rate just under 10% of the total area being deforested annually in the region, although the reforestation rate is on the rise.

The effectiveness of these instruments depend to a large degree on their integration into the overall governmental context, i.e. involving other institutions and feeding into other national and sectoral policies. Generally, though, these laws have emerged in an unarticulated fashion, out of context and without adequate coordination with other sectors of the economy and the public administration. An example of this is the case of Panama, where the Law on Forestry Incentives took a long time to influence the procedures of the Ministry of Finance, and for the institutional arrangements within INRENARE to be organised. This situation was aggravated by the absence of implementing regulations (these were finally adopted five years after the decree on the Law on Forestry incentives).

In addition, specific policies still tend to contradict the new forest laws, by derogating from incentive systems or introducing perverse incentives that promote deforestation and land use changes in areas suitable for forestry. In Nicaragua, for example, the Law for Fiscal and Commercial Justice[23] eliminated the positive incentives created by the Law of the Environment. In Honduras, the Law for the Protection of Coffee Production[24] immunises national and communal lands from agrarian reforms, as well as private property under coffee cultivation in any part of the country regardless of its actual potential. Furthermore, it encourages the destruction of natural forests by authorising coffee producers located in national or communal lands to apply for, and obtain, full property rights from the National Agrarian Institute, if they comply with the requirements established in this decree.

With this background in mind, it can be suggested that clear international rules on forests, providing clear guidelines on timber trade and incentives for forest conservation, would support the conservation policies being attempted, against the odds, by Central American nations. For instance, the sale of environmental services linked to forests cannot become a reality until those countries that pollute the atmosphere the most agree to pay for the benefits provided by the healthy forests in developing countries. This also leads us to think that those countries which produce more pollution are in no position to require developing countries to cease their use of forests, which provides, in the majority of cases, necessities for the livelihood of the poorest segments of the population. It is clear, therefore, while Central America has developed a legally-based incentive system which is more preventive than coercive, it will not able to reach the goals of conservation and sustainable use of forests without the cooperation of the international community.

---

[23]   Decree No. 257.

[24]   Law Decree No. 199-95, in the Official Journal 01-03-1996

Appendix 1

Work Programme for Forest Biological Diversity Under the Convention on Biological Diversity: Decision IV/7 of the Conference of the Parties

The Conference of the Parties,

Recalling decision III/12 of the third meeting of the Conference of the Parties, and recommendations II/1, II/8 and III/3 of the Subsidiary Body on Scientific, Technical and Technological Advice,

Having considered the report of the Executive Secretary on the draft programme of work for forest biological diversity (UNEP/CBD/COP/4/7),

Taking note of views expressed by the Parties and countries on the development of the work programme, as contained in document UNEP/CBD/COP/4/Inf.11,

Noting that the development and implementation of national measures that enhance the integration of the conservation and sustainable use of forest biological diversity into national forest and land-use programmes and forest-management systems is an important task for both developed and developing countries,

Looking forward to the outcomes of forthcoming work under the Intergovernmental Forum on Forests (IFF), including the global workshop on underlying causes of deforestation, to be hosted by the Government of Costa Rica in January 1999,

Reaffirming that the proposals for action contained in the final report of the Intergovernmental Panel on Forests (IPF), in particular those related to national forest and land-use programmes, and the objectives of the Intergovernmental Forum on Forests, provide a good basis for the implementation of key provisions of the Convention on Biological Diversity at the national level,

Noting that decision IV/13 gives further guidance to the Global Environment Facility (GEF) with regard to forest biological diversity,

1. Decides to endorse the work programme for forest biological diversity as contained in the annex to the present decision;

2. Urges Parties, countries, international and regional organizations, major groups and other relevant bodies to collaborate in carrying out the tasks identified in the work programme;

3. Calls upon Parties and countries to integrate forest biological diversity considerations in their participation and collaboration with organizations, institutions and conventions affecting or working with forest biological diversity;

4. Invites the Food and Agriculture Organization of the United Nations (FAO) to further integrate forest biological diversity into ongoing work with the Global Forest Resources Assessment;

5. Urges Parties and countries and international financial institutions, including the Global Environment Facility, to give high priority to the allocation of resources to activities that advance the objectives of the Convention in respect of forest biological diversity;

6. Calls upon the Global Environment Facility (GEF) to provide financial support, in accordance with Article 7 of the Convention, for activities and capacity-building for the implementation of the work programme for forest biological diversity and the use of the clearing-house mechanism, particularly for activities to halt and mitigate deforestation effects, basic assessments and monitoring of forest biological diversity, including taxonomic studies and inventories, focusing on forest species, other important components of forest biological diversity and ecosystems under threat;

7. Invites Parties, when requesting assistance through the financial mechanism, to propose projects that are being fully consistent with previous guidance of the Conference of the Parties and promote the implementation of the focused work programme on forest biological diversity;

8. Requests the financial mechanism of the Convention to consider the operational objectives of the programme of work as a guidance for funding in the field of forest biological diversity and strongly encourages the Global Environment Facility to assist in the implementation of the programme of work at the national, regional and subregional level;

9. Notes the potential impact of afforestation, reforestation, forest degradation and deforesta-tion on forest biological diversity and on other ecosystems, and, accordingly, requests the Executive Secretary to liaise and cooperate with the Secretariat of the United Nations Framework Convention on Climate Change and the Secretariat of the Convention to Combat Desertification in Those Countries Experiencing Serious Drought and/or Desertification, particularly in Africa to achieve the objectives of the Convention on Biological Diversity;

10. Requests the Executive Secretary to compile a synthesized report on the information on forest biological diversity made available to the Conference of the Parties, particularly national reports;

11. Requests the Executive Secretary, in implementing the work programme on forest biological diversity to actively continue collaborating and cooperating with the secretariat of the Intergovernmental Forum on Forests and relevant institutions and to inform the Conference of the Parties thereon;

12. Requests the Subsidiary Body on Scientific, Technical and Technological Advice, in accordance with its mandate, to provide advice on the status and trends of forest biological diversity and the identification of options for the conservation and sustainable use of forest biological diversity to the Conference of the Parties at its sixth meeting;

13. Requests the Executive Secretary to transmit this decision to the Intergovernmental Forum on Forests at its second meeting, to the Conference of the Parties to the United Nations Framework Convention on Climate Change at its fourth meeting and to the Conference of the Parties to the Convention on Desertification at its second meeting.

Annex

WORK PROGRAMME FOR FOREST BIOLOGICAL DIVERSITY UNDER THE CON-VENTION ON BIOLOGICAL DIVERSITY

I. INTRODUCTION

1. In accordance with decision III/12 of the Conference of the Parties, this work programme on forest biological diversity focuses on the research, co-operation and development of technolo-gies necessary for the conservation and sustainable use of forest biological diversity of all types of forests in the programme elements and priority areas already identified.

2. The work programme is based on recommendation III/3 of Subsidiary Body on Scientific Technical and Technological Advice and incorporates the views and interests expressed by Parties and countries. The work programme is action-oriented, demand-driven, needs-driven and flexible enough to reflect and respond to changing conditions, including but not limited to, the outcome of and the priorities to be identified by the Intergovernmental Forum on Forests (IFF). The work programme also reflects the varied needs and circumstances of Parties, indicating that inclusion of

an activity in the work programme does not necessarily imply full participation in that activity by all Parties. In carrying out work under the identified programme elements, Parties should recall the further research priorities listed in recommendation II/8 of the Subsidiary Body on Scientific, Technical and Technological Advice.

A. Objectives

3. The objectives of the programme of work are:

(a) To enhance Parties' abilities to realize the objectives of the Convention through improved implementation, by encouraging and assisting Parties to develop measures for enhancing the integration of conservation and sustainable use of biological diversity into their national forest and land-use programmes and forest-management systems;

(b) To facilitate the implementation of the objectives of the Convention on Biological Diversity based on the ecosystem approach;

(c) To provide an effective and complementary tool to national forest and land-use programmes for the implementation of the Convention on Biological Diversity at the national level;

(d) To identify traditional forest systems of conservation and sustainable use of forest biological diversity and to promote the wider application, use and role of traditional forest-related knowledge in sustainable forest management and the equitable sharing of benefits, in accordance with Article 8(j) and other related provisions of the Convention;

(e) To identify mechanisms that facilitate the financing of activities for the conservation, incorporation of traditional knowledge and sustainable use of forest biological diversity, taking into account that activities should be complementary to, and should not duplicate, existing efforts;

(f) To contribute to ongoing work in other international and regional organizations and processes, in particular to the implementation of the proposals for action of the Intergovernmental Panel on Forests and to provide input to IFF;

(g) To contribute to the access to and transfer of technology in accordance to Article 16 of the Convention; and

(h) To identify the contribution of networks of protected areas to the conservation and sustainable use of forest biological diversity.

B. Time-frame

4. The programme of work reflects a rolling three-year planning horizon in three phases, on the assumption that, in its consideration, the Conference of the Parties will identify a rolling longer-term programme of work.

C. Review and planning process

5. Each phase of the work programme should be subject to periodic review and the development of the work programme, including work in its future phases, should take into consideration recommendations made by the Subsidiary Body on Scientific, Technical and Technological Advice. The phases and outputs should take into account the time-frames and work of IFF.

6. Interim reports after each three-year phase to provide the Conference of the Parties with information on progress made in the implementation of the work programme.

D. Ways and means

7. In its recommendation III/3, the Subsidiary Body on Scientific, Technical and Technological Advice identified the following ways and means for carrying out the work programme: workshops, regional meetings, the clearing-house mechanism, scientific meetings and case-studies. Other feasible ways and means include:

a.   National mechanisms and pilot projects;

(b)   Peer-review mechanisms, including networks of experts or liaison groups and inter-agency task force groups, relying to the extent possible on existing electronic communication systems;

(c)   Use of national and international data and meta-databases, especially in the national and regional monitoring of forest biological diversity;

(d)   Bearing in mind Articles 16 and 17 of the Convention, use of remote-sensing technologies to assist Parties to assess changes in their forest biological diversity, as well as to enhance their ability to report on certain aspects of criteria and indicators frameworks.

E. Collaborative efforts

8. The work programme should support and enhance cooperation on the conservation and sustainable use of forest biological diversity at all levels, ranging from community to inter-organization level, nationally and internationally. At all levels the work programme should be developed and implemented with relevant stakeholders, recognizing that the most important part of work is action at the national level.

9. In the context of this work programme, collaboration should be strengthened in particular with the Convention to Combat Desertification in Those Countries Experiencing Serious Drought and/or Desertification, particularly in Africa and with the United Nations Framework Convention on Climate Change, in order to advance the effective implementation of the Convention on Biological Diversity.

II. WORK PROGRAMME

Elements of the proposed work programme

10. The work programme elaborates, as follows, the elements for inclusion therein.

1. Holistic and inter-sectoral ecosystem approaches that integrate the conservation and sustainable use of biological diversity, taking account of social and cultural and economic considerations

11. The IPF proposal for action 17 encourages countries to develop, implement, monitor and evaluate national forest programmes, which include a wide range of approaches for sustainable forest management, including ecosystem approaches that integrate the conservation of biological diversity and the sustainable use of biological diversity.

Research

Approach

12. Synthesize existing knowledge of holistic and inter-sectoral approaches that enhance the integration of forest biological diversity conservation into sustainable forest management, examine how such integration can be better achieved, and assist in identifying priority research areas in relation to these approaches.

Activities

13. Examination of methodologies for enhancing the integration of forest biological diversity conservation and sustainable use into an holistic approach to sustainable forest management.

14. Development of methodologies to advance the integration of traditional forest-related knowledge into sustainable forest management, in accordance with Article 8(j).

15. Cooperation on the conservation and sustainable use of forest biological resources at all levels, ranging from community to inter-organization level, at the national and international levels in accordance with Articles 5 and 16 on the Convention.

16. Case-studies from countries in which the ecosystem approach has been applied in sustainable forest management practices, including arid and semi-arid areas. This could assist other countries in developing their own national actions and approaches under this work programme.

17. Sharing of relevant technical and scientific information on networks at all levels of protected forest areas and networking modalities, taking into account existing national, regional and international networks and structures, in all types of forest ecosystems.

Ways and means

18. Clearing-house mechanism, national pilot projects, the Convention on Biological Diversity participating in Inter-Agency Task Force on Forests (ITFF) and in the meetings of IFF to actively encourage countries to implement national forest programmes that encompass an ecosystem approach which ensures the maintenance of forest biological diversity values, while also taking into account social, cultural and economic considerations.

19. Consideration of the UNEP guidelines and the FAO document entitled "Basic principles and operational guidelines for the formulation, execution and revision of national forestry programmes" for the preparation of country studies of biological diversity.

20. The integration of social, cultural and economic considerations into the conservation and sustainable use of forest biological diversity will bring the concept close to sustainable forest management. The issue should also be dealt with thoroughly in other forums, mainly within the work under IFF.

Outcomes

21. A better understanding of the ecosystem approach as it relates to forest biological diversity, and an elaboration of the linkages to other work under the Convention, including the incorporation of Article 8(j).

22. Guidance of the Convention on Biological Diversity to IFF and other relevant forums and conventions.

23. Cooperation among Parties and with organizations and conventions.

24. A better understanding of the complexity and interdependencies of biological communities and their dependencies on the abiotic site-specific factors.

25. Methodologies to help ensure that forest plans and practices reflect the social, cultural and economic values of forests as well as the views of forest stakeholders.

26. Identification of general guidelines or methodologies to help ensure that forest plans and practices reflect biological diversity conservation considerations, as well as social, cultural and economic factors.

27. Clarification of the links between the ecosystem approach and sustainable forest management.

Development of technologies

Approach

28. Promote activities to support the development of techniques and means for the effective conservation and sustainable use of biological resources, in particular, full support for technology transfer from developed to developing countries, in accordance with Article 16 of the Convention.

2. Comprehensive analysis of the ways in which human activities, in particular forest-management practices, influence biological diversity and assessment of ways to minimize or mitigate negative influences

Research

Approach

29. Promote activities for an enhanced understanding of positive and negative human influences on forest ecosystems by land-use managers, policy makers, scientists and all other relevant stakeholders.

30. Promote activities to assemble management experiences and scientific, indigenous and local information at the national and local levels to provide for the sharing of approaches and tools that lead to improved forest practices with regard to forest biological diversity.

31. Promote activities with the aim of providing options to minimize or mitigate negative and to promote positive human influences on forest biological diversity.

32. Promote activities to minimize the impact of harmful alien species on forest biological diversity, particularly in small island developing States.

Activities

33. Identification of means and mechanisms to improve the identification and prioritization of research activities related to the influences of human activities, in particular forest management practices, on forest biological diversity.

34. Improve dissemination of research results and synthesis of reports of the best available scientific and traditional knowledge on key forest biological diversity issues.

35. Case-studies on assessing impacts of fires and alien species on forest biological diversity and their influences on the management of forest ecosystems and savannahs.

Ways and means

36. Regional workshops and/or liaison meetings that bring together experts in sustainable forest management, sustainable use and science from the forest sector and, if necessary, representatives from other relevant sectors, with experts on biological diversity, bearing in mind the IPF proposal for action contained in paragraph 94 of the report on its fourth session.

37. The sharing of forest and land-use guidelines, for example, through the clearing-house mechanism, to ensure the fuller integration of genetic, species and habitat diversity into sustainable forest management systems.

Outcomes

38. Analysis of human impacts on forest ecosystems, as well as an enhanced ability to prioritise research needs and apply results and an enhanced understanding of the role of traditional knowledge in ecosystem management to minimize or mitigate negative influences, and to promote the positive effects.

39. Expansion of research capacity to develop and assess options incorporating the applications of traditional knowledge to minimize or mitigate negative influences, and to promote the positive effects.

3. Methodologies necessary to advance the elaboration and implementation of criteria and indicators for forest biological diversity

Research

Approach

40. Foster activities to determine and advance the methodology for elaborating and implementing the criteria and indicators of forest biological diversity. These activities could supplement work that has already been developed. In this regard, coordination with IFF, and drawing upon existing and ongoing work at the national, regional and international levels, is recognized as an important approach.

41. Foster activities to determine criteria and indicators for the conservation and sustainable use and the fair and equitable sharing of benefits arising out of utilization of resources of forest biological diversity and to advance methodology for integrating these criteria and indicators into existing criteria and indicators processes.

42. The work related to indicators of forest biological diversity could also imply the need for an inventory to assess current status and trends in forest biological diversity, at the local and national level based on repeated measures of the selected indicators. The work under this programme element could also include, inter alia, capacity-building on taxonomy and inventories, taking note of the work under the Global Taxonomy Initiative.

Activities

43. Assessment of experiences gained in the national and regional processes, identifying common elements and gaps in the existing initiatives and improving the indicators for forest biological diversity.

44. Taxonomic studies and inventories at the national level which provide for a basic assessment of forest biological diversity.

Ways and means

45. Collaboration with national institutions and relevant bodies and in coordination with the work on the general development of methods for implementing Article 7 under the Convention. Collaboration with ITFF member agencies; cooperating with and complementing existing criteria and indicators initiatives for sustainable forest management, including regional initiatives to develop appropriate criteria and indicators, such as the Helsinki process for boreal, temperate and Mediterranean-type forests in Europe; the Montreal process for temperate and boreal forests outside Europe; the Tarapoto proposal for the Amazon forest; the UNEP/FAO-initiated processes for dry-zone Africa and the Near East in arid and semi-arid areas; and the "Lepaterique" process for Central America initiated by FAO and the Central American Commission for Environment and Development (CCAD). (See background document for the Intergovernmental Seminar on Criteria and Indicators for Sustainable Forest Management, Helsinki, June 1996.) 46. Review of specific indicators of forest biological diversity that have been derived by the major ongoing international processes related to sustainable forest management. The prioritization of related activities should consider the development of indicators that are capable of providing the most useful information on national or regional status and trends of forest biological diversity.

Outcomes

47. Methodologies to advance the elaboration and implementation of criteria and indicator frameworks and the improved capacity of countries to implement these frameworks.

48. Contribution to the national and regional initiatives in the development of indicators under the criteria for forest biological diversity.

4. Further research and technological priorities identified in the recommendation II/8 of the Subsidiary Body on Scientific, Technical and Technological Advice as well as issues identified in the review and planning process under the work programme

49. Included under this element is a series of specific research and technological priorities initially identified under recommendation II/8 of the Subsidiary Body on Scientific, Technical and Technological Advice. These represent important issues brought forward into the Convention from the IPF proposals for action. These priorities are among the issues to be discussed by IFF at its scheduled meetings in 1998 and 1999 and within the inter-sessional meetings of the IFF (for example, the international seminar on research and information needs in international forest processes, to be held in Vienna in September 1998) as part of its attempt to identify and define global and regional research priorities for forests, taking into account national priorities. It is essential that the Convention on Biological Diversity coordinates with IFF in order to enhance synergy on these issues as they intersect with the programme of work for forests under the Convention on Biological Diversity.

50. Following input from IFF on these priorities, the Conference of the Parties may wish to consider incorporating them in phases 2 and 3 of this work programme. When additional scientific and technological priorities are identified, they can similarly be incorporated in the periodic planning activities and reviews of the work programme.

Research

Analysing measures for minimizing or mitigating the underlying causes of forest biological diversity loss

51. Besides unsustainable forest-management practices, there are other causes for the loss of forest biological diversity in forest ecosystems, such as habitat transformation, harmful alien

species, pollution, erosion, uncontrolled forest fires and poverty. There is a need for a better understanding of the underlying social, cultural and economic causes of forest biological diversity loss and the improvement of measures for mitigating those causes.

Assessing ecological landscape models, the integration of protected areas in the ecosystem approach to sustainable forest management and the representativeness and adequacy of protected areas networks

52. Conserving the biological diversity of forests should be carried out both by establishing protected areas and by taking into account biological diversity conservation in all types of forests outside the protected areas, taking into account plantation forests. The outcome of this programme element would include the further development of methods to integrate protected areas into sustainable forest management and analysis of the representativeness and adequacy of the protected areas networks.

53. Reducing gaps in knowledge in the areas of fragmentation of habitats and population viability, to include mitigation options such as ecological corridors and buffer zones.
54. The work should also contribute to the preparation of the discussions of the Conference of the Parties on in situ conservation.

Advancing scientific and technical approaches

Activities

55. Promoting the development of scientific and technical local approaches to:

(a)   Conserve and sustainably manage biological diversity in production forests;

(b)   Rehabilitate degraded and deforested ecosystems as appropriate;

(c)   Enrich indigenous biological diversity in forest plantations.

56. Developing assessment and valuation methodologies for the multiple benefits derived from forest biological diversity.

Decisions IV/1Report and recommendations of the third meeting of the Subsidiary Body on Scientific, Technical and Technological Advice, and instructions by the Conference of the Parties to the Subsidiary Body on Scientific, Technical and Technological Advice IV/2Review of the operations of the clearing-house mechanism IV/3Issues related to biosafety IV/4Status and trends of the biological diversity of inland water ecosystems and options for conservation and sustainable use IV/5Conservation and sustainable use of marine and coastal biological diversity, including a programme of work IV/6Agricultural biological diversity IV/7Forest biological diversity IV/8Access and benefit-sharing IV/9Implementation of Article 8(j) and related provisions IV/10Measures for implementing the Convention IV/11Review of the effectiveness of the financial mechanism IV/12Additional financial resources IV/13Additional guidance to the financial mechanism IV/14National reports by Parties IV/15The relationship of the Convention with the Commission on Sustainable Development and biodiversity-related conventions, other international agreements, institutions and processes of relevance IV/16Institutional matters and the programme of work IV/17Programme budget for the biennium 1999-2000 IV/18Date and venue of the fifth meeting of the Conference of the Parties IV/19Tribute to the Government and People of the Slovak Republic.

Appendix 2

Global Environment Facility: Operational Programme Number 3 on Forest Ecosystems

Guidance

3.1   This Operational Programme responds to the three sets of guidance provided by the Conference of the Parties (CoP) of the Convention on Biological Diversity (CBD) to the GEF as the institutional structure operating the financial mechanism on an interim basis. The first set of guidance is from the first CoP[1] and includes policy, strategy, and eligibility criteria, as well as program priorities among which are the following related to forested areas:

(a)   Projects that promote the conservation and sustainable use of biological diversity...in other environmentally vulnerable areas... [2]; and

(a)   Projects that promote the conservation and/or sustainable use of endemic species.[3]

3.2   At its second meeting, the CoP approved the second set of guidance,[4] concerning inter alia finance for measures for conservation and sustainable use and for *in-situ* conservation,[5] and preliminary consideration of components of biodiversity under threat.[6]

3.3   The second CoP also considered a number of general issues related to forests and biological diversity[7] and highlighted, among other matters, that forests play a crucial role in maintaining global biodiversity;[8] that tropical, temperate, and boreal forests provide the most diverse sets of habitats for plants, animals, and micro-organisms, holding the vast majority of the world's terrestrial species;[9] that the maintenance of forest ecosystems is crucial for the conservation of biological diversity well beyond their boundaries ... providing ecological services and, at the same time, livelihoods or jobs for hundreds of millions of people worldwide;[10] that forests are becoming degraded and their biological diversity is being lost;[11] and that forests and forest biological diversity play important economic, social, and cultural roles.[12]

3.4   Although not specifically directed to the GEF, the second CoP also reaffirmed that "the ecosystem approach should be the primary framework of action to be taken under the Convention"[13] and stressed the need "to identify the driving forces determining the status and trends of

---

[1]   Document UNEP/CBD/COP/I/17, Policy, Strategy, Programme Priorities and Eligibility Criteria for access to and utilization of financial resources of the Convention on Biological Diversity. Annex 1, pages: 33-34.

[2]   Ibid. 4(k).

[3]   Ibid. 4(l).

[4]   A call to Action: Decisions and ministerial statement from the Second Meeting of the Conference of the Parties to the Convention on Biological Diversity. Jakarta, Indonesia, 6-17 November, 1995.

[5]   Ibid. Decision II/6 11, referring to decision II/7 on Articles 6 and 8 of the Convention.

[6]   Ibid. Decision II/6 11, referring to decision II/8, para 2.

[7]   Ibid. Decision II/9 and its annex.

[8]   Ibid. Decision II/9, Annex, para. 3, page 26.

[9]   Ibid. Annex, para 4, page 26.

[10]   Ibid. Annex, para 5, page 26.

[11]   Ibid. Annex, para 7, page 27.

[12]   Ibid. Annex, para 8, page 27.

[13]   Ibid. Decision II/8, para 1.

components of biological diversity."[14] The ecosystem approach is followed in the Operational Programs and identification of driving forces is stressed in biological diversity.

3.5   At its third meeting, the Conference of the Parties (COP) of the Convention on Biological Diversity (CBD) approved additional guidance for the GEF in its capacity as the institutional structure managing its financial mechanism on an interim basis. The guidance is directly relevant to, and can be fulfilled through Enabling Activities, long-term Operational Programs, and/or Short-term Response Measures. In addition, the operational response to the guidance on agrobiodiversity will be consolidated in an operational policy note on the treatment of agrobiodiversity in the context of the four current Operational Programs in biological diversity.

3.6   The Conference of the Parties:[15]

(a)   urged Implementing Agencies to enhance cooperation to increase efforts to improve processing and delivery systems;
(b)   asked GEF to "...provide financial resources to developing countries for country-driven activities and programmes, consistent with national priorities and objectives..."[16] on the following topics: capacity building in biosafety, including for the implementation by developing countries of the UNEP International Technical Guidelines on Safety in Biotechnology; capacity building for initial assessment and monitoring programs, including taxonomy; supporting efforts for the conservation and sustainable use of biological diversity important to agriculture; and for capacity building and country driven pilot projects on the Clearing-house Mechanism (CHM);
(a)   reconfirmed the importance and requested support for incentive measures;
(b)   urged capacity building efforts to implement measures and guidance on access to genetic resources;
(c)   requested GEF to examine the support of capacity building for indigenous and local communities embodying traditional lifestyles;
(d)   requested GEF to incorporate targeted research and promotion of awareness activities when relevant to project objectives and consistent with national priorities; and
(e)   requested GEF to collaborate with the CBD Secretariat in preparing a proposal on the means to address the fair and equitable sharing of the benefits arising out of genetic resources, including assistance to developing country Parties.

3.7   The Conference of the Parties[17] requested GEF to make financial resources available to developing country Parties for urgent implementation of relevant aspects of Articles 6 and 8, which concern general measures for conservation and sustainable use and for *in-situ* conservation.

3.8   The present Operational Program responds to the above decisions.

Program Objective

3.9   The objective of this Operational Program is the conservation and sustainable use of the biological resources in forest ecosystems.

---

[14]   Ibid. Decision II/8, para 3.

[15]   UNEP/CBD/COP/3/38, annex II, Decision III/5.

[16]   Idem, para 2.

[17]   Idem, Decision III/9, paras 2, 3, and 4.

(a)　Conservation[18] or *in-situ* protection, will be sought through protection of primary/old growth and ecologically mature secondary forest ecosystems, by establishing and strengthening systems of conservation areas, focusing primarily on tropical and temperate ecosystems in areas at risk; and

(a)　Sustainable use[19] forest management will be sought by combining production, socio-economic, and biodiversity goals. The Operational Strategy calls for a range of uses from strict protection on reserves through various forms of multiple use with conservation easements to full scale use.

3.10　The key assumptions are as follows:

(a)　Scope. Conservation and sustainable use will be achieved in a variety of specific ecosystems that are identified as priorities within National Biodiversity Strategies or other national plans such as UNCED reports, Tropical Forestry Action Plans, National Environmental Action Plans, etc. Those identified as priorities are likely to be areas of high endemism; of high ecosystem, species, and genome diversity; of high distinctiveness; important for migratory species; important as spawning and nursery grounds; under threat; of high social, economic, cultural, or scientific value; of high productivity; or of a structure and composition shaped largely by natural events and only to a limited extent by human disturbance. For in-situ conservation of areas of importance there is also a large body of work identifying forested areas that should be conserved to represent major habitat types and their species[20]; and

(a)　Replication. Successful outcomes will be replicated elsewhere on the basis of the experience and learning gained.

Expected Outcomes

3.11　A successful outcome is one where globally important biodiversity has been conserved or sustainably used in a specific forest ecosystem.

Monitoring outcomes

3.12　Outcomes would be monitored and evaluated by measuring key indicators of ecosystem structure and function, and of sustainable use. Examples of monitoring and evaluation methodologies and tools include:

(a)　surveys of forest cover, including measures of the age and species on managed stands; other measures of the population of native species, showing these to be high enough to be viable in-situ; and

---

[18]　GEF Operational Strategy, Chapter 2, pages 17-18.

[19]　Idem, pages: 18-19.

[20]　Examples of key publications for identifying specific sites at the regional level are: in the Latin America and Caribbean region, the BSP regional analysis and the WWF/World Bank eco-regions work; in Africa, the World Bank's ecological sensitive areas and IUCN's Conservation Atlas of Tropical Forests; and in Asia, IUCN's review of protected areas systems in the Indo-Malayan region and the Conservation Atlas of Tropical Forests. International (e.g., Ramsar and World Heritage) and regional (e.g., Western Hemisphere, Barcelona, etc.) conventions include the identification of global and regional priority sites for conservation of biodiversity and biological resources.

(b)   measures of the population of key alien, invasive species;

(c)   surveys of organisms or surveys of their parts extracted (e.g., leaves, roots, nuts, seeds, gums, resins, skins, internal organs, etc.,

(d)   ecological surveys within protected forest areas, showing the presence and abundance of indicator or keystone species; and

(e)   measures of the quality of the processes (e.g. water quality, nutrient cycling, etc.) that maintain the integrity of the ecosystems.

Assumptions and risks to achieving the outcomes

3.13   A key assumption is that Implementing Agencies, in their regular work programs, will assist countries to analyse the causes[21] of biodiversity loss at the ecosystem level, which could include demographic and economic factors, and to identify and implement national plans that address such root causes. Supplementing this baseline course of action, GEF can assist with additional actions to address driving forces or proximate causes of biodiversity loss and unsustainable use.

3.14   There are some risks to achieving successful outcomes at the ecosystem level through conservation and sustainable use activities and these risks will be addressed through emphasis on good project design. The following important risk-reducing steps will need to be confirmed in project proposal documents:

(a)   Complementarity. The necessary complementary activities, such as expected policy changes and the availability of bilateral and other sources of finance, will take place;

(b)   Size and corridors. The protected forest area and the necessary connecting corridors are large enough, and the practice of sustainable use of resources in the surrounding productive landscape is widespread enough, to ensure that the most threatened and endangered components of forest biodiversity will be protected; and

(c)   Absorptive capacity. The absorptive capacity of agencies and NGOs to implement the GEF activity and all the other activities necessary for protecting the ecosystem and use available funds effectively.

Project Outputs

3.15   Outputs of GEF projects and related forest ecosystems activities would be monitorable. Examples include:

(a)   Protected areas. Well established systems of forest conservation units with effective management plans;

(b)   Threat removal. Removal of the causes of biodiversity loss and the specific threats to the ecosystem arising in the surrounding productive landscape, e.g., through reduced encroachment;

(c)   Sectoral integration. Incorporation of biodiversity protection into the main productive sectors of the economy; and integrated community development addressing livelihood issues of local and indigenous communities living in the buffer zone and areas of influence of protected areas;

(d)   Sustainable use. Sustainable logging and other forest industries; and

(e)   Institutional strengthening. Stronger institutions and well-trained staff to address these issues.

---

[21]   World Resources Institute, 1992. Global Biodiversity Strategy, pages: 12-18.

GEF Activities

3.16   GEF can support[22] investment, technical assistance, capacity building (institutional strengthening, human resource development, and information exchange, including participation in the Clearing-house Mechanism), policy, public education, and targeted research. Through these means, GEF will help to finance the conservation of biodiversity and sustainable use. [23]

3.17   Typical conservation activities are:

(a)   demarcating, gazetting, strengthening, expanding, and consolidating protected forest areas, and maintaining forest corridors within the main productive landscapes, particularly in areas that are critical habitats or of importance for migratory species;

(b)   assessing the impact of natural disturbances and the compound effects of anthropogenic stress;

(c)   remedial actions in forest under threat;

(d)   control of alien, invasive species;

(e)   capacity building for biosafety activities formulated on a case-by-case basis in the context of a specific project responding to country-driven national priorities;

(f)   identifying components of biological diversity important for its conservation with regard to the indicative list of Annex I of the CBD;

(g)   identifying processes and categories of activities which have or are likely to have significant adverse impacts on the conservation of biodiversity;

(h)   piloting selected activities that are country-driven national priorities and which develop and/or test methods and tools, such as rapid biological/ecological/social assessment, geographic information systems, and data analysis systems of importance for the conservation of biodiversity;

(i)   demonstrating and applying techniques to conserve biodiversity important to agriculture, such as wild relatives of domesticated plants and animals;

(j)   supporting capacity building efforts that promote the preservation and maintenance of indigenous and local communities' knowledge, innovation, and practices relevant to conservation of biological diversity, with their prior informed consent and participation;

(k)   incorporating components for targeted research important for biological diversity conservation, when relevant to project objectives and consistent with national priorities; and

(l)   including sustainable use awareness components when relevant to project objectives and consistent with national priorities.

3.18   To maintain biodiversity and the diversity of biological resources, GEF sustainable use activities will be supported in forest ecosystems. Sustainable development activities that integrate biodiversity and biological resource concerns are central to and a necessary foundation for national sustainable development goals. Typical GEF sustainable development activities would be in areas surrounding critical habitats that require integration of biodiversity protection and sustainable development in sectoral plans. In addition, consistent with the incremental cost approach, GEF could pay for activities that could be modified specifically to protect biodiversity. Typical examples are:

(a)   integration of biodiversity conservation and sustainable use objectives in land use and natural resource use management plans;

---

[22]   GEF Operational Strategy, Chapter 2, Biodiversity, pages: 17-21.

[23]   GEF Operational Strategy, Chapter 2, Biodiversity, pages 16-17 under forest ecosystems.

(b)   integrated pilot projects providing alternative livelihoods to local and indigenous communities residing in buffer zones of globally important biological areas;

(c)   integrated conservation and development projects around protected forests;

(d)   participatory management of natural resources, and alternative livelihoods;

(e)   tenure reform and land titling in the buffer zones around important protected forests;

(f)   sustainable production and use of natural products (e.g., sustainable forest management practices;

(g)   improvement in rural and community wood-lots specifically to remove pressure on fuelwood obtained from protected forests; adjusting sustainable logging regimes to protect natural habitats of global significance; intensification of agricultural productivity in surrounding areas to minimize encroachment on marginal forested areas of high biodiversity value;

(h)   establishment of long-term cost recovery mechanisms and financial incentives for sustainable use;

(i)   capacity building for biosafety activities formulated on a case-by-case basis in the context of a specific project responding to country-driven national priorities;

(j)   identifying components of biological diversity important for its sustainable use with regard to the indicative list of Annex I of the CBD;

(k)   identifying processes and categories of activities which have or are likely to have significant adverse impacts on the sustainable use of biodiversity;

(l)   piloting selected activities that are country-driven national priorities and which develop and/or test methods and tools, such as rapid biological/ecological/social assessment, geographic information systems, and data analysis systems of importance for the sustainable use of biodiversity;

(m)   demonstrating and applying techniques to sustainably manage biodiversity important to agriculture, such as wild relatives of domesticated plants and animals;

(n)   supporting capacity building efforts that promote the preservation and maintenance of indigenous and local communities' knowledge, innovation, and practices relevant to conservation of biological diversity, with their prior informed consent and participation;

(o)   incorporating components for targeted research important for biological diversity conservation when relevant to project objectives and consistent with national priorities; and

(p)   including sustainable use awareness components when relevant to project objectives and consistent with national priorities.

Project risks

3.19   Project proposals would also address the main risks to being able to reach the desired outputs by:

(a)   Best practice. Using and adapting best practice for GEF activities, and best available knowledge to establish the necessary baseline and indicators to monitor impacts; and

(b)   Local communities. Ensuring that local communities accept and respect the boundaries of protected forests and the limits imposed on biological resource extraction; scaling up and expanding successful community development activities; encouraging the active participation of local communities, NGOs, and other key stakeholders; and incorporating the knowledge of local and indigenous communities.

Inter-Agency Coordination

3.20   The activities would be coordinated with the past, ongoing, and prospective work of the Implementing Agencies and others. These will include experience gained, lessons learned, and dissemination of experience from the Pilot Phase activities, and the experience of multilateral, bilateral, and private institutions, the international and national NGO community, and international, regional, and national research centres and academic institutions.

Land Degradation

3.21   Global and nationally significant forested lands have and are suffering substantive land degradation in the form of deforestation and desertification. The GEF will fund pilot activities that prevent deforestation and promote sustainable use and sustainable management of forests and forested areas at risk in order to conserve their biodiversity.[24] Pilot rehabilitation and restoration activities will be supported on tropical and temperate forest ecosystems in areas at risk (e.g. with threatened and/or endangered species and ecosystems).[25]

Public Involvement

3.22   It is one of ten basic operational principles for the GEF that its projects will provide for consultation with, and participation as appropriate of, the beneficiaries and affected groups of people. The GEF Council approved a paper on Public Involvement in GEF-financed Projects that defines the procedures for information dissemination, consultation, and stakeholder participation, including the following:

(a)   that there should be emphasis on local participation and local stakeholders; and
(b)   that specific conditions in-country should be taken into consideration.

3.23   These principles respond to the guidance of the CoP.[26] Strategic partnerships will be sought, where possible, among all relevant stakeholders (e.g., government, NGOs, academia, the private sector, local communities, and indigenous groups), each group collaborating based on comparative advantage. Projects to implement the Operational Program will clarify the conditions of cooperation and transparent mechanisms to ensure the active participation of relevant stakeholders in the planning, implementation and monitoring of project activities.   Partnerships will be appropriate to local conditions and build on local expertise.

Resources

3.24   GEF resources will be used to meet the incremental costs of activities in this Operational Program. The financial resources required over the period of the first three years are estimated to be between US $ 160 and 185 million. This includes resources for unforeseen short-term-responses that offer quick and cost-effective measures.

---

[24]   GEF Operational Strategy, Chapter 2, Biodiversity, page 11.

[25]   Idem, page: 16 under Forest Ecosystems.

[26]   Decision II/6, para 10, page 22 and Idem, Decision III/5.

Appendix 3

1993 Regional Convention for the Management and Conservation of the Natural Forest Ecosystems and the Development of Forest Plantations
(Central American Forest Convention)

CONSIDERING:

That the Tegucigalpa Protocol, which institutes the Central American Integration System (SICA) reaffirms, among its objectives "To establish concerted actions directed to the preservation of the environment through respect and harmony with nature, ensuring a balanced development and rational exploitation of the region's natural resources with the perspective to establish a New Ecological Order in the region."

That the forestry development potential of Central America is based on its existing 19 million hectares of natural forests and in its 13 million hectares of lands with forestry potential that are presently without forests;

That the wealth and diversity of the different life zones and species found in the region's tropical forests, linked to its isthmic nature, as a bridge between the continental masses of North and South America, make this Central American Region the most important deposit of genetic wealth and biological diversity in the world;

That, in contrast with this wealth, there is another reality: at present, more than 20 million Central Americans live in poverty conditions, particularly those 14 million that live in extreme poverty conditions since they cannot even satisfy their basic needs of nutrition. It is important to point out that two thirds of the poor live in rural areas;

That, every day, in the region, it becomes more evident that poverty worsens forest and local environmental degradation, and increases even more with the external debt and the loss in the terms of exchange, all products of an unbalanced growth in the previous decades;

The in the rural sector, the concentration of land is even greater than what the indices show since, frequently, the best lands are occupied by those that have the means and technology to exploit them, relegating the poor to poor quality land, basically on the hill sides. This is the habitual cause for deforestation and the high levels of erosion and soil loss observed in the region, which lead to an even greater empoverishment of those who work these areas;

That a frontal attack on poverty is a fundamental part of the restructuring and modernizing strategies of the economy.

This strategy requires the massive incorporation of technical progress in productive efficiency and greater social equity, to increase the quality of life of this poor majority, and to facilitate and support their absolute access to the productive and investment processes and to increase their productive performance;

That forest resources which cover 45% of the regional territory, and the soils with forestry potential, which add up to 60% of the region, must play a prevailing role in this strategy;

The despite this potential, it is estimated that about 416,000 hectares per year are deforested (48 hectares per hour), at a rate that increases over time;

That deforestation in the upper watersheds has provoked erosion, floods, drought, losses in the agricultural and forestry potentials, and losses in biodiversity, whose joint effects limit the development opportunities and worsen rural poverty, thus reducing the quality of life of Central Americans;

That the high levels of external indebtedness and the subsequent debt service charges reduce the possibility of long-term investment, particularly that which is associated with the sustainable development of natural resources and, rather, increases the pressure on them and on the soil resource which runs the risk of over-exploitation for the production of high input and short-term crops which can generate the foreign exchange required to service that debt;

That the potential of the Central American forests to produce goods and services is not being value in its just dimension, nor is it used in a rational and sustainable manner. The genetic diversity, the scenic value, their potential to produce timber and non-timber goods can be the basis for not only conserving forest resources, but also for making them contribute, in a significant and sustainable manner, to abate underdevelopment in Central America;

That the forest resource must contribute to increase the quality of life of the Central American people through the fostering and promotion of national and regional actions conducive to decreasing its loss, ensuring its rational use and to establish the mechanisms required to revert the process of its destruction.

AGREE ON THE FOLLOWING CONVENTION:

CHAPTER I
FUNDAMENTAL PRINCIPLES

Article 1
Principle

According to the United Nations Charter and the principles of international law; the signing States of this Convention, reaffirm their sovereign right to proceed to use, manage and develop their forests in agreement with their own policies and regulations, as a function of:

a.   Their needs for development.
b.   Conserving and sustainably using their forestry potential as a social and economic function.
c.   Ensuring that the activities under each control and jurisdiction, do not cause environmental damages to the country nor to other countries in the region.
d.   Strengthening the application of policies and strategies contained in the Forestry Action Plans of each of the Member Countries. Therefore, the Convention and its derived Programs must not affect the activities that each country is carrying out in its forest areas, nor its access to financial resources from international agencies.

Article 2
Objective

The objective of the present Convention is to promote national and regional mechanisms that will prevent a change in land use of those areas covered with forests that are occupying lands with forestry potential, and to recover those deforested areas, to establish a homogeneous soil classification system, through the reorientation of settlement policies in forest lands, the discouragement of actions that propitiate forest destruction in lands with a forestry potential, and the promotion of a land-use planning process and of sustainable options.

CHAPTER II
POLICIES FOR THE SUSTAINABLE DEVELOPMENT OF THE FOREST RESOURCE

Article 3

The Contracting States of this Convention commit themselves to:
a.   Maintaining the options open to sustainable development for the Central American countries, through the consolidation of a National and Regional System of Protected Wildlands, that ensure the conservation of biodiversity, the maintenance of vital ecological processes, and the utilization of sustainable flows of goods and services of their natural forest ecosystems.
b.   Orienting national and regional agricultural programs, under an integral vision, where the forest and the trees constitute a basic element of productivity and the soils are used

according to their best aptitude.

c. Orienting national and regional forest management programs under a conservationist view, where:
    i. The rehabilitation of degraded and secondary forests has high priority since they constitute an abundant forest mass in the region, with an already established infrastructure, which represent a great potential for improving the standard of living for two thirds of the poor that live in the rural areas.
    ii. The management of the primary natural forests acts as a buffer to stop or reduce pressures to their conversion to other land uses.
d. Orienting national and regional reforestation programs to recover degraded lands, preferably of forestry aptitude and presently under agricultural use, such that they can provide multiple uses to different land users, giving preference to the promotion of native species, and to the local participation in planning, implementation and distribution of benefits. These programs must give priority to the supply of fuelwood for domestic consumption, and to other forest products of local community use.
e. Making the necessary efforts to maintaining a dynamic large-scale inventory of the forest cover in the countries of the region.

CHAPTER III
FINANCIAL ASPECTS

Article 4

The Contracting States of this Convention must:
a. Propitiate the creation of Specific National Funds such that, since the moment they are conceived, they can financially support national priorities identified on the basis of the objectives outlined in Chapter II.
b. Create mechanisms that ensure there-investment of income generated by the forest resource (timber use, ecotourism, potable water supply, hydroelectric production, biotechnology, and others).
c. Create mechanisms that, according to the possibilities of each country, ensure credit access to groups such as ethnic groups, women, youth, civic associations, local communities, and other vulnerable groups, in a manner such, that they can develop programs according to the features of this Convention. This should also be applicable to specific national funds such as those in the system of financial intermediaries already in existence.
d. Strengthen international negotiating processes (commerce, external debt administration, bilateral and multilateral cooperation) such that they can channel financial resources destined to strengthen these funds.
e. Propitiate the necessary methodological modifications in the System of National Accounts in each country, that will allow for the introduction of environmental parameters that will allow for the value and depreciation of forest resources and soils in estimating the economic growth indicators in each country (the Gross National Product).
f. Establish mechanisms to avoid the illegal traffic of flora and fauna species, timber and other products. Particular emphasis should be dedicated to the control of illegal commerce in the border areas between countries of the region.

CHAPTER IV
POPULAR PARTICIPATION

Article 5

The States of the Region must:
a. Promote the participation of all interesting parties, including local communities and indigenous populations, private enterprise, workers, professional associations,

nongovernmental organizations, and individuals, and the inhabitants of forested areas, in the planning, implementation and evaluation of national policy resultant from this Convention.

b.   Recognize and duly support the cultural diversity, respecting the rights, obligations and needs of indigenous peoples, their communities and those of the other inhabitants of forested areas.

CHAPTER V
INSTITUTIONAL STRENGTHENING

Article 6

The Contracting States of the present Convention must:

a.   Strengthen the sectorial and inter-sectorial coordinating mechanisms in order to impel sustainable development.

b.   Strengthen the forestry development institutional framework in each country, through the adoption of the National Tropical Forestry Action Plans, as mechanisms to reach the objectives of this Convention.

c.   Create environmental attorney general's offices in the legal framework of each country, that will watch for the protection and improvement of the forest resource.

d.   Create, by law, through the respective legislative powers, the obligation to carry out environmental impact studies in forest areas where large scale forestry concessions, or other economic activities are being proposed, that may have a negative impact on the forest.

e.   Profit from the comparative advantages of each country, propitiating their transfer to the rest of the countries.

f.   Strengthen the region's technical capacity through training and applied research programs, and the promotion of forestry techniques in productive and planning activities.

g.   Data on infrastructure and necessary means to ensure quantity and quality of forestry seeds that may be needed.

h.   Data on the personnel necessary for the vigilance and conservation of national forests.

CHAPTER VI
REGIONAL COORDINATION

Article 7

The Central American Commission on Environment and Development (CCAD) is instructed to implement a Central American Council on Forests in conjunction with the National Administrations of Environment and Development, integrated by Forest Service Directors of each country, the National Coordinators of the Tropical Forestry Action Plans, or the authority designated by each State, who together will have the responsibility of the follow-up of this Convention.

Article 8

CCAD is given the mandate to request support from international organizations or friendly governments, in order to fund coordinating activities for the implementation of this Convention.

CHAPTER VII
GENERAL RESOLUTIONS

Article 9
Ratification

The present Convention shall be submitted to ratification by the signatory States, according to the internal standards of each country.

Article 10
Adherence

The present Convention remains open to the adherence of other States of the Mesoamerican Region.

Article 11
Deposit

The instruments of ratifications or of adhesion and denunciation of the present Convention and its amendments, shall be deposited and registered in the General Secretariat of the Central American Integration System (SICA), who will communicate them to the Chancelleries of the rest of the Contracting States.

Article 12
State of Being in Force

The present Convention shall be in force on the date the fourth instrument of ratification has been deposited. For each State that ratifies or adheres to the Convention, after the fourth instruments of ratification has been deposited, it will be in force, for that State, on the date its instrument of ratification is deposited.

Article 13
Registration in the United Nations

When this Convention and its amendment are in force, the General Secretariat of SICA shall proceed to send a certified copy of these, to the General Secretariat of the United Nations, for the purposes of registration that are indicated in Article 102 of this Organization.

Article 14
Denunciation

The present Convention shall be denounced when any Contracting State so decides. The denunciation shall have effect, for the denouncer State, 180 days after it has been deposited and the Convention shall continue in force for the rest of the States, as long as at least three of them remain adhered to it.

IN WITNESS WHEREOF, the present Convention is signed in the City of Guatemala, Republic of Guatemala, on the twenty ninth day of the month of October, nineteen ninety three.

List of Acronyms

AIJ	Activities Implemented Jointly
ALIDES	Alliance for Sustainable Development
C&I	National Level Criteria and Indicators
CBD	Convention on Biological Diversity
CCAB	Central American Council on Forests
CCAD	Central American Commission on Environment and Development
CCAP	Central American Council for Protected Areas
CCD	UN Convention to Combat Desertification in Countries Experiencing Serious Drought and/or Desertification, Particularly in Africa
CDM	Clean Development Mechanism
CIFOR	Centre for International Forestry
CITES	Convention on International Trade in Endangered Species of Wild Fauna and Flora
COP	Conference of the Party
COFO	FAO Committee on Forestry
CSD	Committee on Sustainable Development
CTE	Committee on Trade and Development
DPCSD	UN Department for Policy Coordination and Sustainable Development
EIA	Environmental Impact Assessment
EU	European Union
FAO	Food and Agriculture Organisation
FCCC	UN Framework Convention on Climate Change
FCP	Forestry Capacity Programme
FDI	Foreign Direct Investment
FINNIDA	Finnish International Development Agency
FSC	Forest Stewardship Council
GATT	General Agreement on Tariffs and Trade
GEF	Global Environmental Facility
GNP	Gross National Product
IBRD	International Bank of Reconstruction and Development
IDA	Finnish International Development Agency
IFC	International Finance Corporation
IFF	Intergovernmental Forum on Forests
ILO	International Labour Organisation
IMF	International Monetary Fund
INRENARE	Institute for Renewable Natural Resources
IPCC	Intergovernmental Panel on Climate Change
IPF	Intergovernmental Panel on Forests
IRENA	Institute for Natural Resources
ISO	International Organisation for Standardization
ITFF	Inter-agency Task Force on Forests
ITTA	International Tropical Timber Agreement
ITTC	International Tropical Timber Council
ITTO	International Tropical Timber Organisation
IUCN	International Union for the Conservation of Nature and Natural Resources
MAB	Man and the Biosphere
MAI	Multilateral Agreement on Investment
MIGA	Multilateral Investment Guarantee Agency
NAFTA	North American Free Trade Agreement
NBS	National Biodiversity Strategy
NFP	National Forest Programmes
NGO	Nongovernmental Organisation

OECD	Organisation for Economic Cooperation and Development
PAF-CA	Tropical Forest Action for Central America
PARLACEN	Central American Parliament
PPM	Production and Processing Method
SBI	Subsidiary Body on Implementation
SBSTTA	Subsidiary Body on Scientific Technical and Technological Advice
SICA	Central America Integration System
SIDA	Swedish International Development Agency
SFM	Sustainable Forest Management
SPS	Agreement on the Application of Sanitary and Phytosanitary Measures
STRP	Scientific and Technical Review Panel
TBT	Agreement to Technical Barriers to Trade
TFAP	Tropical Forestry Action Programme
TFRK	Traditional Forest-related Knowledge
TRIPS	Agreement on Trade Related Aspects of Intellectual Property
TRIMS	Agreement on Trade-Related Investment Measures
TWG	Timber Working Group
UN	United Nations
UNCED	UN Conference on Environment and Development
UNDP	UN Development Programme
UNEP	UN Environment Programme
UNESCO	UN Educational, Scientific and Cultural Organisation
UNDESA	UN Department of Economic and Social Affairs
UNCTAD	UN Conference on Trade and Development
UNGASS	UN General Assembly Special Session
USAID	United States Agency for International Development
WHC	Convention Concerning the Protection of the World Cultural and Natural Heritage
WTO	World Trade Organisation
WWF	World Wildlife Fund